I'LL GO
WHERE YOU WANT ME
TO GO

JOHN & SUSANNAH,

I GIVE THIS BOOK TO YOU TO READ
AND GAIN AN UNDERSTANDING OF THE JOY
THAT COMES TO THOSE WHO CHOOSE TO
SERVE AS SENIOR MISSIONARIES. MAY IT
INSTILL WITHIN YOU A DESIRE TO SOMEDAY
GIVE OF YOUR TIME AND TALENTS AS
SENIOR MISSIONARIES.
OFA ATU

Douglas W. & Sandra C. Banks

I'll Go Where You Want Me to Go

Published by Douglas W. and Sandra C. Banks
Edited by Daniel Friend of Precision Editing Group
Interior and cover design by EpubMasters

ISBN: 978-1492183969

Printed in the United States of America
Year of first printing: 2013

ACKNOWLEDGMENTS

We have been blessed to have many friends and family members who have given unselfishly of their time and talents with the many versions of this book. It is difficult to properly express our gratitude for their help in bringing this book to fruition. We are particularly grateful to Raquel Garfield who went beyond the call of duty in making detailed comments and Joan Bybee for her kind remarks and comments. We are thankful for the wise counsel from our son Jared and daughter Marla Cluff about various approaches to the style of the book. We also received invaluable comments from our dear friend Ken Carlson, who did the first painful reading of the beginning of the early chaotic manuscript. Jo Scoffield was a giant helper in closing out the preparation of the book for printing.

We express sincere gratitude to the professionals who assisted; Daniel Friend of the Precision Editing Group for his conscientious editing comments and suggestions; Rachel Ann Nunes for giving us extremely insightful counsel and advice about the design, cover and publishing process.

We are especially thankful to our granddaughter Kensington Cluff who took time from her valuable school studies to do the proof reading of the final document. A special thanks also goes to our granddaughter Hannah Panek.

CONTENTS

Preface

❖

We have many friends that have served as senior missionaries. We have been grateful and deeply touched by their unselfish service given all over the world. We have heard many reports on their missions in sacrament meetings and firesides. Some of their numerous and diverse assignments included working in temples, teaching seminary and institute, serving as missionary doctors, working in mission offices, administering the Perpetual Education Fund, serving in branches (teaching, training, and activating), mentoring and helping people upgrade job skills and enhance employment, teaching in Tonga's Liahona High School and coordinating humanitarian services. They served in a variety of locations including Connecticut, California, Mexico, Belarus, Israel, Malaysia, Kenya, Chile, Peru, Tonga, Greece, Ecuador, and Navaho Indian Reservation.

As we have listened to our friends' senior missionary accounts, we realized that many of the experiences were common to all senior missionary service, but we also realized that each mission is unique, with special challenges and opportunities that stretch and test you. While many of their accounts were unique we realized that our mission to the Tonga Nuku'alofa Mission had been especially unique. Our mission account was more than knocking on doors and preaching the gospel. It is a captivating story of meetings with a King; losing the mission president overboard in the ocean during a turbulent storm; facing a gripping drought; the miracle of learning a language; helping a people of faith be a people of programs and procedures; the harrowing evacuation of an injured missionary; and other rare missionary experiences. I believe that our account will help people to understand that senior missionary work is never boring! There are new challenges and new adventures every day.

In our search to learn about senior missionary service we found no biographies or novels concerning senior missionaries and we feel that more Church members need to hear some of these amazing stories. This book is for the senior missionaries who have served and will yet serve. It is our hope that it will rekindle memories, recognize common experiences and challenges; and also give prospective senior missionaries a taste of what they may experience. We hope you enjoy reading about our mission as much as we enjoyed living it.

Most of all it is our desire that this biography will help to instill in mature members of the Church a desire to give of their time and talents to senior missionary service. Our own personal feelings about senior missionaries are best expressed by President Gordon B. Hinckley who said: "As I have thought of this man and woman [senior missionaries] who left the comforts of home and society and friends at an age when most people want to slow down and take it easy, I have thought of the words of the Lord, 'And every one that hath forsaken houses, or brethren, or sisters, or father, or mother, or wife, or children, or lands, for my name's sake, shall receive an hundredfold, and shall inherit everlasting life.' (Matthew 19:29.) I have thought the same whenever I meet or hear of other elderly brothers and sisters, single or married, who either volunteer or accept calls to serve the Lord in the missions of the Church.

"We need them. The Lord needs them. The people of the earth need them. And those wonderful brothers and sisters also need that blessed experience. For, generally speaking, the most miserable people I know are those who are obsessed with themselves; the happiest people I know are those who lose themselves in the service of others." (President Gordon B. Hinckley, "Whosoever Will Save His Life", *Ensign*, Aug. 1982, 4–5)

A Mission Call with a Surprise

❖

We need many older couples, who, in general, are retired and have reared their families. There is a great work for them to do as official missionaries. . . . Many of our good people have reared their families and settled down in advancing years and have relaxed to enjoy life without selflessly sharing it.

President Spencer W. Kimball, Regional
Representatives seminar, 30 Sept. 1977, 11–12

Our desire to serve as a full-time missionary couple did not come through a sudden impulse or inspiration. It was a strong desire that built over a long period of time. For many years we had heard requests from the prophets, seers, and revelators for couples to serve missions. Even before we were born, President Heber J. Grant, in the General Conference of October 1925, had issued a clarion call for mature individuals of sound judgment and experience in preaching the gospel to labor in the mission field. (Conference Report, Oct.1925, 10.) President Spencer W. Kimball had repeatedly asked for more missionary couples and we felt that we should follow the prophets' calls and "do it."

Elder David B. Haight, in his April 1979 conference address, issued this challenge to couples: "Some stakes are crowded with mature couples fully prepared to accept a mission call, who could not only enthusiastically help in spreading the gospel but strengthen new members in areas of the world where we are growing so rapidly. The thousands of newly baptized members now in the Church, with its somewhat strange, unfamiliar ways, could be encouraged and trained by someone who today is sitting comfortably at home." (Elder David B. Haight, "Feed My Sheep," *Ensign,* May 1979, 62)

Sandy and I made the decision to serve a mission together more than twelve years before we actually filled out our missionary papers and met with our local leaders. We planned how we would prepare to serve and calendared the time when we would submit our missionary papers. Planning a long time in advance helped us overcome the major concerns of most senior missionaries, known as the four *f*'s: fear, family, fitness and finances.

Our plan was for me to retire at age 57, the earliest age when my retirement pay could actually begin. This would reduce our retirement income, but we felt that it would still be adequate because of other financial plans. Part of this plan included the sale of our nice, big, beautiful home so that we did not have to worry about the large mortgage payments it required. We even planned the date that we would put the house on the market and estimated the time it would take to sell the house.

Everything went well until the large accounting firm that I was part of merged with another. With this merger came a request that I, a long-time tax partner, leave the firm. This was a shock to my ego and a big hit on my wallet, and I spent some time feeling sorry for myself. After exploring many opportunities, including teaching at a university, joining another accounting firm, or taking a job in the corporate community, I determined to establish my own tax consulting practice and signed a five-year lease on a large office space, which pushed our plan to serve a mission back a couple of years. This experience taught us there is need for flexibility in plans to be a senior missionary.

The work change turned out to be a blessing. I found more freedom in my life, which allowed me to serve as a temple ordinance worker with Sandy. There was an adjustment to a reduced income, but the only long-term downside of the change was the delay in our missionary service.

In 1997, as the lease on the office space began its final year, I arranged to sell my tax consulting practice to an employee. Sandy and I then placed our house on the market during one of the worst times the area residential market in the Northern Virginia area had ever seen. Sandy, however, was confident that the house would sell in a short period of time. Her faith was rewarded when the house sold in about a month. Then another surprise occurred when the proposed sale of my tax practice fell through. The challenge was soon overcome when a good friend, John Behrens, a fellow CPA who knew of our mission plans, came to me and inquired about merging our practices. This "tender mercy" helped pave the way for us to serve a mission. While our merger agreement was being finalized, we submitted our missionary papers. We were cutting it pretty close. Luckily, we did not have any complications with doctor or dentist, which can frustrate potential senior missionaries.

I had served a mission from 1957 to1960 in the Tonga Nuku'alofa Mission. I was the missionary replacement for Elder John H. Groberg when he returned home. Unlike Elder Groberg, I did not serve on Niuatoputapu, the island memorialized in *"The Other Side of Heaven"*, but spent my entire mission away from the main island of Tongatapu. I was what they called at the time a *"bush Elder."* I also didn't have the adventurous trip to the mission that he did, but it did take me 16 days to arrive in the mission. I travelled by boat from San Francisco, California, to Suva, Fiji, and then to Nuku'alofa, Tonga.

As I had served my mission in Tonga, or the "Friendly Islands," as it was called then, I noted on the missionary papers that I spoke Tongan. I indicated that although it had been almost 40 years since I had used the Tongan language with any frequency, I thought that I could pick up the language quickly. Sandy said that I was making a statement of a desire to serve in Tonga, but I didn't believe so. We were not asking for any particular missionary service, and we knew that non-Tongan couples had never been sent to Tonga as proselyting-leadership missionaries. We felt that we would be called to be proselyting-leadership missionaries because of our good health and so-called "youth."

Not long after our missionary papers were submitted to the

Missionary Department in Salt Lake City, Sandy was called out of town to Madison, Wisconsin, to help with the birth of our new grandson. We determined that I would not open the mission call if it came while she was gone, and we decided to hold a conference call with all of our children when we did open it.

Sandy traveled to Madison, and the calls came in two separate envelopes. Some strange thoughts ran through my mind as I contemplated this. We had assumed that the call would come in a joint letter to both of us, but there were two letters in the mailbox. Could it be possible that we had been called to different missions? Was only one of us called and the other rejected? I called Sandy immediately, and we arranged a specific time for a conference call with all of our six children, who were living in three different time zones. I was tempted to peek at the letter, but I fought off the temptation and waited until the conference call. Five hours later I opened the letter and read the mission call from the prophet. I started to read the letter, but as I saw where we had been called to serve, my emotions overcame me. It took all the strength I could muster to say, "Tonga Nuku'alofa Mission" through my tears of joy and excitement. Everyone was saying, "Oh, my gosh! Wow! I can't believe it!" It was a wonderful surprise.

Preparing to Go

❖

Just being there and being available is a tremendous blessing . . . The couple's experience weighs heavily in their behalf. Often they teach part-member families and reap the rewards of seeing people baptized, families united in the Church. And while good health and a sound financial foundation are important, the most vital requirements may be love and a willing heart.

Vaughn J. Featherstone, "Couple Missionaries: 'Too Wonderful for Me,'" *Ensign*, Sept. 1998, 14–17

While our lifetime spent raising our family and serving in the Church helped us prepare to serve as missionaries, we knew that the most vital requirements might be willing minds and loving hearts. We often asked ourselves, "Are we prepared for this?" We found our answer in a quote from Elder Neal A. Maxwell: "God does not begin by asking us about our ability, but only about our availability, and if we then prove our dependability, he will increase our capability!" (Elder Neal A. Maxwell, *The Neal A. Maxwell Quote Book,* Bookcraft, Inc., 1997, 1)

We had received and accepted our mission call, but we had fewer than eight weeks to arrange the move. Our call arrived in the second week of November 1997, and we were to report to the Missionary Training Center (MTC) on January 6, 1998. Not only would we have to prepare for the mission, but we would also have to deal with the Thanksgiving, Christmas, and New Year's holidays. It was a very busy time. We raced to make radical changes in our life. We would be leaving behind relationships, careers, the city we lived in, and the old versions of ourselves. We would put on our missionary mantle and continue growing and moving forward and all of this change was not without some fear and pain.

As we began our preparation in earnest, I thought my situation paralleled Lehi leaving Jerusalem after he received a message from the Lord. Our mission call was a message from the Lord to go into the wilderness of Tonga. The scripture says, ". . . he departed into the wilderness. And left his house and the land of his inheritance, and his gold, and his silver, and his precious things." (1 Nephi 2:4) I drew this parallel because the scriptures tell us that we should "liken all scriptures unto us, that it might be for our profit and learning," (1 Nephi 19:23) and I knew that I would profit from such an analysis. As I did, I found comfort in these words of the Lord to Lehi: "I will also be your light in the wilderness; and I will prepare the way before you, if it so be that ye shall keep my commandments." (1 Nephi 17:13) I realized that, like Lehi and the Israelites, wandering in the wilderness could teach us better than anything else about our absolute dependence on God.

Physical Preparation

Because we were going to be out of the country for 18 months, we had to deal with many issues at a rapid pace. Our to-do list was long, but the time to accomplish everything was short. One of the major items that needed immediate attention was finding someone to live in our house for 18 months. We had just sold our large home in anticipation of serving a mission and purchased a smaller and newer home. None of our children lived close or could make a move to Virginia to live in our house while we were in the mission field, so we began hunting for tenants. Then another tender mercy of the Lord occurred when a young, childless couple moved into our ward. The wife had served as a sister missionary in our ward and, in fact, had lived in our home for a period during her missionary service. We knew her and felt comfortable with them, so we worked a nice arrangement for them to live in our home at a substantially discounted rent for the 18 months that we would be gone. It was a great relief to have this settled.

Now, in the winter, we had to find clothes for the warm weather of Tonga. For men, this is not too difficult, but for women it's another story. The main difficulty for me was finding short-sleeved white shirts, while for Sandy it was finding lightweight cotton dresses and shoes. Sandy had many conversations with the mission president's wife and the mission president's secretary discussing what we should bring. While a package we received from the MTC did provide a list of suggested items, it was invaluable to talk to people who were currently there and experiencing the weather.

"Missionary Immunization/Preventive Medication Requirements" also took time and attention. We needed vaccinations for hepatitis A and B, tetanus, diphtheria, tuberculosis, measles, mumps, rubella, and more. We also needed mammogram screening, PSA testing, and blood tests. The list went on and on, and it seemed like it would never end. Some of these items were required by the missionary department. Others were visa requirements. We also had to ensure that our medical insurance would cover us during our mission overseas. Ours did not so we changed to the Church's medical insurance.

Our financial affairs were a major focus of our preparation. We needed to update our will and grant legal and medical power of attorney to an agent to prepare for any unforeseen emergencies. We were fortunate to have a number of attorneys in our family, and our daughter, a CPA, was already doing our taxes for us. We authorized her to take care of our various banking, pension, and investment affairs. Accomplishing the drafting and signing of these various items was complicated by the fact that she lived in Utah and we were in Virginia. We also had to determine how she would transfer money to us and whether we would set up a bank account in Tonga or just write checks from our local bank account. We learned that it cost money to cash foreign checks in Tonga so this had to be factored into our decision. We recognized that attention to financial details up front would let us focus on the work in the mission field.

There were a number of other little items that required attention, including making sure our driver's licenses didn't expire while we were abroad, arranging with the post office and various companies to have mail forwarded to our daughter, and making plans to communicate with our loved ones at home. We determined that we would take our laptop computer with us to help with our communications with our family by email. We did not know at the time that we would spend more than two thirds of our mission in an area without internet access. We did learn that we would need a power transformer and special adaptors on our computer to take care of the local variance in the electricity. We were able to borrow the transformer from the mission, but since we did not have internet we transmitted our letters by copying them onto computer disks and sending them to the mission office which would email the messages to our family. We tried to think through all these details as best we could. Once we did, we did not fear because we knew that Lord would help us take care of anything truly essential.

As the day of our flight to the Provo MTC drew nearer, I kept putting off clearing out my business office to let someone else take over. It was still not completed on the day we were to fly to the MTC. I went to my office with what I thought was plenty of time to pack all the loose items and bring them home in boxes to store. Our flight was at one in the afternoon, and when I left to clean the office out I had not yet packed many of my winter clothes for the week we would spend in the MTC. It was noon when I arrived home from the office with my packed boxes. I thought we had only one hour before the flight left. Although we did not have to contend with hour-long waits at security checkpoints in 1998, we still needed to arrive on time. I expected when I arrived home that Sandy would have put out a suitcase for me to pack so that I could do it quickly. I ran into the house, but Sandy was not home. No suitcase had been put out for me to pack my things. I was now in a state of panic. I rushed to the basement to find a suitcase. All of our family was home except Sandy and Jeff, and the others informed me that the two of them had gone to the store and were not yet back. I was now breaking out in a cold sweat. I expected at any moment to have chest pains and fall over with a heart attack. Then I heard my daughter laughing. I didn't think this was anything to laugh about. She then informed me that the flight had been delayed for two hours because of some mechanical problems. When Sandy arrived home from her short shopping trip, she had a good laugh—though I was still pretty stressed. It was a learning moment for me as Sandy taught me how procrastination has its natural consequences. We would not have made it to the airport on time without the tender mercy of a delayed flight.

Spiritual Preparation at the MTC

Now that we had completed our physical preparations we went to the MTC in Provo, Utah to be polished for full-time missionary service. Although training time for senior missionaries has varied over the years, we spent two weeks at the MTC. We were housed in a motel a short driving distance from the main MTC facilities, but all of our training took place on the MTC campus. The MTC training moved at a spiritually exhausting pace. The instructors sought to develop our spiritual literacy by helping us understand the true meaning of various gospel principles and how to apply them in our missionary service. There was so much good knowledge and information being presented to us that we didn't have time to think about everything we were learning. Someone has said "it's like trying to drink out of a hose that's shooting water. You can't get it all, but what you get is wonderful." The information at the MTC was coming out of a fire hose rather than a garden hose.

The MTC became a fountain of living water in which we quenched our righteous thirst. The Savior taught, "Blessed are they which do hunger and thirst after righteousness: for they shall be filled." (Matthew 5:6) Clearly, all the missionaries at the MTC had a great thirst for righteousness and sought to be filled. (See Revelations 21:6; Psalm 42:1–2)

We attended devotionals; we were instructed on teaching the missionary discussions and taught some of them to local volunteers; we received instruction about reactivation and met with more volunteers to have discussions about it; we had lectures on retaining new members, making appointments, extending commitments, finding people to teach, principles of leadership, giving service, and many other skills and doctrines that would help us to be better senior missionaries. We even had instruction on disease prevention.

One of the most uplifting parts of our MTC experience was meeting the other senior missionaries and learning about their personal histories and their decisions to serve missions. We met couples preparing for various types of missionary work, from temple work to office work to farm work. These couples came from all walks of life, various occupations, and diverse Church experiences, but they all had a common desire to answer the call of the prophet by serving a mission and a deep, abiding love of God and their fellow man. They were enthusiastic and dedicated.

Almost as suddenly as the MTC experience began, it was over, and we were cast out of a spiritual like bubble into the lone and dreary world. We thought it was a small taste of what Adam and Eve experienced when they were cast out of the Garden of Eden.

A Busy First Month

You are making a sacrifice, but it is not a sacrifice because you will get more than you give up, you will gain more than you give, and it will prove to be an investment with tremendous returns. It will prove to be a blessing instead of a sacrifice. No one who ever served this work as a missionary, who gave his or her best efforts, need worry about making a sacrifice because there will come blessings into the life of that individual for as long as he or she lives.

President Gordon B. Hinckley, *Teachings of Gordon B. Hinckley*, Deseret Book Co., 1997, 356

We arrived in Tonga by way of Hawaii, where we arranged a day-long layover so that we could visit our daughter and her husband, who were attending BYU-Hawaii. We not only had an opportunity to visit with them but to attend the temple and the Polynesian Cultural Center, as well as visit with Eric and Carolyn Shumway. Eric had served with me in Tonga as a young missionary and is a legend there because of his great knowledge of the language and the culture. He was then serving as a Vice-President of the BYU-Hawaii but was soon to be inaugurated as the president of the university. We paid a price for the visit—the plane from Hawaii left at 3:15 a.m. and arrived in Tonga six and a half hours later.

President Alfred and Jane Malupo were at the airport to greet us and prepare us for the beginning of an exciting and uplifting eighteen-month experience. President Malupo informed us that we would remain in Nuku'alofa until our housing accommodations in Ha'afeva were completed.

We were then taken to a nice duplex unit where we dropped off our baggage. We began taking the steps necessary to establish Tongan residency, which included applying for a driver's license and establishing a bank account. We also bought a few groceries to get started. Fred and Patty Nielson, the mission office couple, were assigned to acclimate us to the country. Fred was from Bluewater, New Mexico, and we had been acquainted as students at BYU. It was a surprise to meet him in Tonga. This was the beginning of a new wonderful friendship as couples which still thrives today. Fred was not at the airport to welcome us because he was in Ha'afeva looking at the schoolhouse and determining how it could be converted to living accommodations for us. We were beginning a major change in our lives. Elder and Sister Nielson did their very best to make it a soft landing, but there were many new things for us to learn as missionaries in Tonga.

Tonga where we would now be serving consisted of three main island groups, Tongatapu, Ha'apai and Vava'u, plus Niuafo'ou and Niuatoputapu—two remote northern island groups. There are 170 islands in Tonga, of which only about 40 are inhabited. The total population of Tonga when we arrived was about 110,000 people, and the population of the Lulunga Governmental District where Ha'afeva was located was just over 2,000 people on 10 small islands.

The growth of the Church in Tonga has been very strong and is one of the great stories of missionary work in the Church. We were glad to be a part of it. Church membership was nearing 50% of the country's population. We would start our mission living on the island of Tongatapu where approximately two-thirds of the nation's population resided. The density of the Church population on Tongatapu was like many of the large cities in Utah; the island is home to 12 of the 16 stakes in Tonga. Every village has a chapel with pillared walkways around the building and a fenced-in combination basketball, volleyball and tennis court at the side which was really an outdoor cultural hall. The buildings are simple yet beautiful structures of white concrete cinderblock with louvered windows and concrete-slab floors.

Getting Acclimated

We had been advised in the MTC that we would face some physical challenges as we adjusted to our new way of life, especially in regards to the diet. Sure enough, during the first few weeks our bowels became very loose, and we had to make sure that we didn't venture too far from restroom facilities. We also had to become accustomed to the various "little creatures" that existed in this new environment. We were familiar with many of these creatures but not their size. In one of our earliest letters home we sent a bug report of a dead cockroach that was one and a half inches long and a spider that was two and a half inches long. We had many "geckos" in our house, and instead of watching TV we observed their behavior on our walls. We found pigs running around outside like dogs do in the US. Pigs are the symbol of Tonga and play an important part in the food chain. One thing we were thankful for was that there are no snakes in Tonga.

Another acclimation challenge was learning how to drive a van on the left side of the road when the steering wheel was on the right side of the van. The real trick was with the turn signal and the windshield wiper levers; they were on the opposite sides from American-built cars, so I frequently turned on the windshield wipers by mistake when I turned a corner. That was a habit that was very difficult to change in only one month of driving in Tonga.

A Funeral

During our first week in Tonga, I started searching for an old missionary companion, Sione Akau'ola Fifita. I found that he was in the village of Vaini, so we went to visit him. We couldn't call ahead because few people there had telephones. We found his home by asking people in Vaini. Only his wife, Pauline, and Sione's mother, Ana Fifita, were at home—Sione was in America visiting some family. We found out later that he was also undergoing prostate cancer treatment. Pauline was in a wheelchair, sick with breast cancer. She didn't look very well. Ana Fifita had helped take care of me as a young missionary on the little island of Koloa in Vava'u. Pauline was sick, but in Tongan fashion gave us two pineapples as a welcome gift. (A symbol of welcome in our home state of Virginia also.) We told them that we would come back in a week when Sione came home from the States.

We returned to Vaini in a week as promised, but as we neared the home it was obvious that someone in the family had died. Everyone was dressed in black and wrapped in the large, old, ragged mats that people wear during a wake. Sione came out to greet us. He informed us that his wife had died that morning, just a day after he'd returned. He said that she had been waiting for him to come home so that she could die. He informed us that the funeral would be at 8:30 the next morning and invited us to attend.

We arrived 15 minutes early to the funeral, but the service had already commenced because all of the family and Church leaders were ready and in place. The chapel and cultural hall were full, so we entered the back of the cultural hall. Sione evidently had been watching for us because as soon as we arrived he came to the back to greet us and escort us to the front of the chapel. We sat with all the family as the funeral service continued. We were a little embarrassed to arrive late, but that didn't matter to Sione. After the wonderful service the members and family gathered outside the chapel and loaded the body in a van draped with tapa cloth. We accompanied the family to the cemetery.

Unlike American funerals, the body was not placed in a coffin, but was laid out on mats with tapa cloth and lace over it. It took eight men to lift and carry the awkward lifeless body from the chapel to the van. The van slowly pulled away from the chapel. We all held the tapa that extended out of the open back of the van as we walked the half-mile to the cemetery. There, we saw that a large cement box had been poured in a large hole in the ground. After the dedication of the grave, the body was placed in the cement box, and corrugated tin was placed over the top. While we waited and watched, fresh cement was poured into a frame on top of the tin, sealing up the cement box. A special reverence permeated the entire simple process. Pauline's funeral was the first of many we would participate in during our mission. For Sandy, it was an introduction to Tongan funeral culture.

The next week we went back to check on Sione to see how he was doing, but he was not at home. We were told that he was at the cemetery erecting the framework to display a beautiful white satin puff quilt with the name *"Pauline"* quilted on it. Pauline herself had made most of it before she passed away. We visited Sione at the cemetery. He hadn't known that his wife had made it, being as sick as she was.

The traditional Tongan grave does not have a headstone. Instead, decorations are placed on framework that's erected at the site. One of our favorite graves was one with dark beer bottles placed in the ground, mouth first in the sand, and white coral in two rows around the gravesite. The graveyard burial mounds, covered with artificial flowers and white pieces of coral, are one of the predominant features of the landscape in Tonga. Handmade quilts add a decorative touch to many graves, while others are marked with flags and banners and surrounded with seashells, flowers, and black volcanic rocks. All of these mounds are scaled-down versions of the *langi*, or nobility grave sites that have been erected for centuries.

An Early Example of Tongan Faith

Tongatapu had been experiencing a drought before we arrived, which had continued during our first month in Tonga. At the end of that month, we were fortunate to have Elder Vaughn Featherstone of the Area Presidency visit the mission, and we had the opportunity to hear him speak both at a zone conference and at a Sunday evening bi-stake fireside. During the luncheon feast in connection with the zone conference, Sandy sat next to Elder Featherstone and instructed him on how and what to eat. You would have thought that she had been in Tonga her whole life. The Bishop of the ward providing the food stood up to speak during the luncheon and said, in traditional Tongan fashion, "We took this assignment because we needed the blessings, and we knew that if we did, rain would come." The night before the zone conference and feast, it began raining, and it rained during most of our meetings that day. This was an early example of the marvelous Tongan faith that we would experience throughout our mission.

Renewing an Old Relationship

When I was a young missionary in Ha'apai, Sio "Joe" Tu'ilatai Mataele, his wife, Alice Brown, and their three children lived in a little one-room corrugated tin house just across the street from our missionary home. Even though they didn't have many material possessions at the time, they were always sharing things with us missionaries. Alice had since died, and Joe became less active. He had been remarried twice and had fathered a number of children outside of marriage. He now lived in Nuku'alofa with his third wife and some of his children. He had become very prominent in Tonga, having been elected to Parliament a number of times, serving as the steward of the wharf, and becoming a close friend of the King. We caught up with him easily because of his prominence, everyone knew him and where he lived. We found it interesting that he was also currently the president of the Planned Parenthood of Tonga and had traveled all over the world to attend their meetings. We inquired how he could hold that position with as many children as he had. Along the way he had fathered over forty children. He told us he could be the president because he could afford to have that many children and Planned Parenthood was about affording the children you had.

We invited Joe to come to Church with us, and he did. It had been a very long time since he had attended Church. Afterwards, he invited us to come over to his house for a roast pig dinner. His wife happened to be out of town attending a banking school. When she returned home a week or so later, she was shocked to discover that he had attended Church. His wife Iona, a Seventh - day Adventist, said, "Thank the Lord! He must be a good friend; I haven't been able to get you to Church." She had promised Joe that if he stopped smoking and drinking she would investigate the Church. Before we left for Ha'afeva, we made arrangements for them to be taught. I told Joe that my goal was to attend the temple with him and Iona before we left the mission field in seventeen months.

We saw Joe and some of his children several times on trips back from Ha'afeva, and he attended Church sporadically throughout our mission. He even bore his testimony in a fast and testimony meeting that his wife attended.

In one of the meetings he attended there was a little problem in a genealogy class, however. They looked up Joe's name in the computer, and it listed eight different women as mothers of his children. Although the computer accurately listed them not as wives, but as mothers of his children, the whole thing embarrassed Iona. The senior missionary running the computer, not understanding what had happened, asked Joe if he had had eight wives. Joe's wife knew all about the other women he'd lived with, but it was still embarrassing to have it in the computer for the entire world to see. Apparently, his active children or someone else had put it into the Church genealogy system. Joe definitely needed to do some repenting, but he was at least starting to come to Church.

While we were in Tongatapu on one occasion he attended Church two Sundays in a row. He and one of his daughters came to regular services one Sunday, and then he and Iona with a couple of other children came to a six stake regional conference to hear Elder Richard G. Scott of the Quorum of the Twelve and the new South Pacific Area President, Elder Quentin L. Cook. Joe and Iona had the opportunity to meet Elder Scott after the meeting. We also met twice with Joe at his restaurant. Joe was making improvement, but he still had a ways to go.

While we were serving on our mission one of his daughters joined the Church, but Joe never became fully active and Iona was never taught. Almost ten years later I received a call from a mutual friend informing me that Joe had passed away and that Joe had become involved in the Church again and that Iona had been baptized. To know of Joe's reactivation and Iona's baptism made us feel that our reactivation and missionary effort had been worthwhile.

Early Missionary Work

We gained a friendship with our neighbors by the duplex, gave them some missionary instruction, and invited them to hear us speak in Church. The husband accepted our invitation and came with a daughter but not his wife. He had a brother in Ha'afeva, where we were going, who was a leader of the Church of Tonga for the Lulunga Group. A number of years later he became the national president of the Church of Tonga. We felt very good about our first month of missionary activities with limited ability in the Tongan language.

Audience with the King

One Saturday afternoon, President Malupo arranged for us, Elder and Sister Nielson, their visiting daughter, and a group of twenty young full-time missionaries to have an audience with the king of Tonga, Taufa'ahau Tupou IV, at the royal palace. The president and his counselor accompanied us. At the request of the palace household, we brought with us some food from a designated restaurant in town. We then waited in the wings while the king ate the shrimp, lobster, and other food we brought. When he was finished, we were invited into his presence. The young missionaries were not invited into the palace, but sat on the nearby veranda and observed and sang. The king was a very large man, but he had lost a lot of weight recently through an exercise program. In fact, he had been working out just before we arrived, so he received us in his sports shirt, tennis shoes, and bright red sweat socks. We sang some songs and read a scripture. President Malupo offered a prayer. We exchanged a few pleasantries and then left. This memorable experience is not common for missionaries.

Ready for the Transfer

It was now the middle of February and we'd obtained all the items we needed to take to Ha'afeva: two dressers, an ironing board, curtain fabric, a little washing machine, and a propane gas stove and oven. We also took a transformer to change the electrical current from 220 to 110 so that we could operate our computer and other electrical equipment. Most of these items were sent ahead by inter-island boat. We flew from Tongatapu to Pangai, Ha'apai. From Pangai we took the small missionary boat with a forty horsepower outboard motor to Ha'afeva. Very rough seas made what should have been a two-hour trip take four hours.

I'll Go Where You Want Me to Go

◆

The refrain, "I'll go where you want me to go, dear Lord"
(Hymns, 1985, no. 270), should be more than a hymn
we sing on Sunday. It should be our own prayer of faith
as we serve wherever the Lord has need of us.

David B. Haight, "Couple Missionaries—A
Wonderful Resource," *Ensign*, Feb. 1996, 6–12

How often I have sat in Church on a Sunday and sung, "I'll go where you want me to go, dear Lord." It is much easier to verbalize the words than to put them into practice. Little did we realize when we wrote our acceptance letters what was meant by "over mountain or plain or sea." We arrived in Nuku'alofa, Tonga, on January 20, 1998, to receive the news from our Mission President, Alfred Malupo, that we would be serving on the stormy sea in Ha'afeva, one of the small islands in the Ha'apai group of islands. I would serve as the district president of the Lulunga District, a district consisting of six branches located on six small islands with populations of only 150–500 people each. Each of these islands was surrounded by sparkling, jewel-colored reefs and waters of black-blue depths, which provide an unforgettable contrast. This would be our home and our work for the next ten months. We learned that anticipating this first mission assignment was as frightening as the anticipation of learning where our mission call would take us.

There was no missionary housing for a couple in Ha'afeva, so the Physical Facilities group, or the PBO, as we called them, was modifying part of an old primary school building into suitable accommodations. The building was being divided into three rooms —a bedroom, a guest bedroom, and a combination living room, dining room, and kitchen. We would also benefit from the addition of indoor bathroom facilities, a propane stove, and a solar panel on the roof to heat water.

It was not until we arrived at the island that we learned that our water would not come from a well but instead from a cistern. The missionary couple house was ten feet behind the chapel and was fenced in as part of the Church house property. The chapel was fitted with gutters and pipes to carry the rainwater from the chapel roof to the cisterns. The main cistern was concrete and about twenty-five feet long, eight feet wide, and seven feet deep. It was connected to two smaller metal secondary cisterns. Standing next to the cisterns was a twenty-foot-high tower with a large tank on top to store the water that was pumped from the cistern. This would provide some water pressure to move the water to the chapel restrooms and the new missionary couple housing. Every house in the village had a cement cistern next to it with small gutters on the roof to catch the valuable rainwater. We would learn over the next ten months just how valuable this water was. They also placed gutters on our small missionary couple house roof with the runoff going to the cistern of our next-door neighbor, a less-active member named Siliote. It seemed like a strange thing to do at first, but this later proved to have been done with great foresight.

We learned on arrival that there was no electricity on the island, but the Church did have a diesel-operated electric generator for the missionary couple's home and the chapel and tennis court. We would run the generator in the evenings for a few hours to pump water from the cistern to the water tower and for the missionary housing lighting and Church activities.

Our stove and refrigerator would be propane operated with a gas cylinder located inside the house. This was the only true stove on the island. Everyone else used the traditional ground ovens called *umu* for baking. This is an oven in the ground with heated rocks and coconut husks burning; banana leaves on top and then the food. The *umu* is covered over with banana leaves and burlap sacks and dirt, or if they are really progressive, a piece of tin. They also had outdoor fireplaces for cooking. The propane cylinders were shipped in by boat as needed.

Ha'afeva consisted of one long, sandy dirt road through the middle of town that ran from one end of the island to the other—about a distance of one mile. Houses lined this road for about one quarter of a mile. There were no automobiles and no horses and carts. Most of the produce from the village farms was carried in gunny sacks on the backs of the farmers. Unlike my earlier mission, every house was now on a wooden or cinderblock foundation and not coconut-leaf thatched.

There was a fence around the village to keep the pigs inside the village and away from the farming area. It was unusual to see that the pigs were not fenced in a pen but instead fenced into the village. When pigs got out into the farming areas, they ruined the gardens. The pigs were very destructive as they rooted up the soil looking for bugs. Occasionally someone would leave the Church gate open, and the pigs would get inside the Church lot and destroy our Church lawn.

Another little oddity was that the people literally window-shopped. The little stores, which carried only a small selection of items on six or seven shelves, did not stay open regular hours. If you wanted to buy something, you would just go to the store and call the owner's name, and they would come out and open the store for you. Two of the store owners lived right next to the stores, but two did not, so you had to go to their house and ask them to open the store. As a result, you literally peeked in the windows to see if they had what you wanted. If they did, you asked them to open up. If not, you tried another store.

We did eventually receive a small washing machine, but the laundry would still be partially done by hand. Sandy only used about half the water possible in the washer, but that meant that the agitator wouldn't work because it wasn't covered with water. She would wash the clothes by scrubbing them in the washer, then putting them in the spinner and having the water returned to the washer to reuse it. She then put the clothes in a bucket of plain water to rinse them, then put them back in the spinner to get the water out and reuse it. At first, she hadn't figured out how to use the machine this way, and it took longer and was not nearly as efficient. She eventually worked out a system to be able to soak and then wash some of the clothes during the day and then finish in the evening when we had electricity to use the spinner.

It did mean that she had to hang the clothes out at night, but she still enjoyed that. It was generally cool and quiet outside, and the sky was so absolutely wonderful and magical with the beautiful crescent moon and the bright stars above. There was almost always a soft, gentle breeze blowing through the beautiful coconut palms. Some nights the clouds played peek-a-boo with the moon. We were so close to the beach that we could hear the music from the breakers roaring on the reef with the changing tide, as well as the gentle little waves lapping upon our sandy shore. They were like two sections of a symphony orchestra. Sandy often said how wonderful it was to be able to look up into the sky amid the beauties of those nights and see the Southern Cross and be reminded of Him for whom we were doing this great work who had created all this for our pleasure and enjoyment. We would enjoy these overwhelming, awe-inspiring views throughout the remainder of our mission.

Learning the Language—A Gift

❖

I learned that . . . the gift of tongues is very real and very much alive in the Church today. I learned that the gift of tongues is much more than just saying or understanding words; it involves deeper understanding that comes from a divine source far beyond mere words. I learned that this gift involves lots of hard work, hours of study and a degree of discomfort, even pain that tests our resolve almost to the breaking point.

Elder John H. Groberg, *In the Eye of the Storm*, Bookcraft, Inc., 1993, 67

One of the challenges we faced with being sent to the island of Ha'afeva was that we would need to develop a quick working knowledge of the language in order to be able to communicate with the people. I had some knowledge, but it had been almost forty years since I had spoken the language on a regular basis. There were no opportunities to speak Tongan in Virginia since there were no Tongans in our area. For Sandy, it meant starting from scratch. When we inquired about language training at the MTC we were told that they did not teach Tongan because they did not currently send young non-Tongan missionaries to Tonga.

The wife of a former North American mission president told Sandy that people her age couldn't learn a language. This individual obviously had not heard Elder Robert L. Backman speak at the October 1992 General Conference when he said, "Some have an idea that as we get older we can't learn languages. That is not true. Again and again, we see couples come to the Missionary Training Center without prior knowledge of a language and leave two months later able to communicate. Of course their skills increase as they love and serve in the mission field. Even when a new language is difficult, older couples perform a unique service in the missions simply by being there. Their experience, example, and faith serve as tremendous resources in building inexperienced members of the Church. They are absolutely indispensable to the growth of the kingdom across the world."(Elder Robert L. Backman, "The Golden Years", *Ensign*, Nov. 1992)

Elder Russell M. Nelson also told senior missionaries that they "need not fear . . . learning a new language. Much can be contributed using talents already acquired. Missionaries can venture into another language situation knowing that they will learn what they need to know without demanding fluency of themselves. They will learn some of their mission language and find joy in using each new expression." (Elder Russell M. Nelson, "Senior Missionaries and the Gospel", *Ensign*, Nov. 2004)

We didn't get two months of language training at the MTC. All they arranged for us was for a young Tongan sister who had served a mission in Japan to spend a couple of afternoons with us, but that was it. Not a very good beginning with the language. In Hawaii we got copies of a Tongan language textbook that Eric Shumway had prepared for Peace Corp workers. When we arrived in Tonga we purchased a Tongan-English Dictionary by Maxwell Churchward.

One thing we did know was that one of the greatest gifts of the Holy Ghost was the gift of tongues. While Sandy's patriarchal blessing did not mention it specifically, the scriptures admonish us to seek after every good gift. The Apostle Paul told the Saints, "Forasmuch as ye are zealous of spiritual gifts, seek that ye may excel to the edifying of the Church." (1 Corinthians 14:12) We understood that through a mixture of diligent study and the aid of the Lord we could acquire the language, so we began a process of diligent study, fervent fasting, and zealous prayer to learn the language rapidly. Our desire was to edify the Church in Ha'afeva and the Lulunga District.

Other than the gift of tongues, we learned the language through two basic means: reading the Book of Mormon together and letting children teach us.

Twice or more each day we would sit together with our Tongan and English copies of the Book of Mormon and go through the slow, laborious process of reading and interpreting. One of us would read a verse from the Book of Mormon in Tongan and then translate it into English. The other would then read the verse in English. If there was a word that we did not understand, we would circle it and write its meaning in the margin. When we translated verses we were familiar with, the translations came easier, as knowing a few Tongan words gave us a hint to the full translation. We learned to translate "and it came to pass" very quickly. One day as we were reading the Book of Mormon we realized that by the time we finished reading it all the way through, we would have read it three times—once in Tongan, once in our own translation, and once in English.

The children were a great help, especially to Sandy. They loved to teach her how to say things and how to understand what they were saying. They were very nonjudgmental and kind, unlike the many Tongan adults who expected her to know the language. They had great love but had no pity for her. They had great faith that she would learn the language . We interacted with the children when school got out each day and on the weekends when they came to our home to put puzzles together and play games.

But the truth of the matter was that we were blessed with the gift of tongues. I often teased Sandy that she was learning the language quickly because I was a great teacher, but we both knew that the real teacher was the Holy Spirit.

Sandy' expressed her thoughts about learning the language in one of her letters home: "This 'humility' thing is pretty tough! It would certainly be a simpler thing if the Lord would just perform a miracle here and give us the gift of tongues as well as soften the hearts of all the people here. He is wise, though, and we are learning lessons in the process and hopefully doing some good. We both agree that the problem with being senior missionaries in these circumstances is that first of all there is no 'native' companion to make the people feel more at ease, and, secondly, that no one really thinks seniors need help. 'I'm sure in their minds we have had so much experience that what could they do to help? That is probably the most frustrating thing . . . so far no one has shown any real interest in 'helping' us. Right now it is especially discouraging, because so many of the regulars here are gone to Tonga [Tongatapu]. Hopefully, they will come home soon. In the meantime, on Friday of one week when we were reading the Book of Mormon in 2 Nephi 30 and 31, it talks about the fact that we must seek and be worthy of the Holy Ghost, and if we don't have it, it is because we are not living worthy of it. That, in [conjunction] with one of the videos we watched about studying the scriptures, really struck me. I have had kind of a down week, and this made me realize again that it's *my* problem—not Dad's, not the Lord's, not a mistake to send us here—but a need for me to repent, humble myself, study the scriptures more, study the language using a prayer first, pray more individually, and open myself up more for the Holy Ghost to work. This is a very difficult assignment, but we are still sure we are where we should be. It would have been easier to stay home and 'hang out,' but this is what we should be doing. We really appreciate your love and prayers."

I had spoken the language fluently some forty years ago, but I also had to start back at the basics and work forward. It was a profound experience to have words that I hadn't used in decades suddenly come to my mind. I remarked to Sandy that this must have been how the Prophet Joseph Smith felt when he received revelation.

Sandy noted down words she heard at meetings. Afterwards, we would figure out the word and its meaning. As time passed, she began to hear words instead of just sounds. One challenge Sandy faced was her high-school Spanish occasionally resurfacing in the midst of her speaking Tongan. We prayed each day for a miracle with Sandy and the language. She began to offer the family prayer with a combination of Tongan and English, and it was not long before she could say the blessing on the food without mistakes. I commented in a letter to the children that "the Lord must laugh when he sees us high five after she says a prayer without mistakes." Soon after, she started to identify things that people said. One evening after our family prayer, which I offered in Tongan, she thanked me for remembering her in my prayer.

I remarked that I would now have to be more cautious in what I said in my prayers. When she gave her first talk in the ward we attended, she wrote out the talk in English and our neighbor Fanongo and I helped her translate the talk and pronounce the words. She did very well with the first of many talks that she would give over the next eighteen months.

As you learn a language you learn about the culture of the people who speak it. The family is central to Tongans. Everyone knows each other's genealogy. They know exactly who is a cousin, brother, or sister to someone else. Tongans are all one giant family, and everyone helps each other. One difficulty we had was that relatives often use the word for "brother" or "sister" to refer to male and female cousins, which caused us problems on a number of occasions. Sandy would often understand that people were brothers or sisters because someone had used the word *tokoua*, or brother. She would even ask two or three times to make sure she was right. I had not remembered from my early missionary years how the word was being used, so we did some research and, through talking with people, finally came to understand the dual use of the word, though we never determined why it was used this way. It made for a very interesting understanding of some relationships until we got things straightened out.

One Sunday when we visited the Matuku Branch, we had a wonderful spiritual experience related to Sandy's language development. Sandy was called upon to say a few words in Sacrament Meeting, which generally happened whenever we visited a branch. She stood and gave her testimony, and it was as if she had been transfigured into a Tongan woman as she spoke. I had to look twice to make sure that it was her speaking. She admonished the people to hold all of their meetings, especially Primary. It was a miracle. She had been doing well before, but it was as if suddenly, she had been blessed with a special gift to sound like a Tongan. It was not as spectacular as the transfiguration of Brigham Young when he spoke to the Saints and it was as though Joseph Smith was speaking, but it was a very beautiful, spiritual, and uplifting experience for both of us. It was a miracle like Elder Dallin H. Oaks spoke of when he said, "We do not usually speak of spiritual gifts as a miracle, but sometimes the effect of a spiritual gift is miraculous. For example, many missionaries who must learn a new language are blessed with the gift of tongues. Most often this gift merely accelerates the normal process of learning, but sometimes its effect is so immediate that it can only be called a miracle. "(Elder Dallin H. Oaks, "Miracles," *Ensign*, June 2001) For me, this miracle was a sign that Sandy would now progress in the language in leaps and bounds.

Sandy's Home Economics

The one "pearl of wisdom" that I might impart to you is how valuable every experience in life is. We have been amazed at how many times, since we have been here, that we have grasped onto some idea or skill we learned along the way. Mom's "basic" cooking lessons have helped me to creatively use what we have here.

Sister Mary N. Cook, First Counselor in the Young Women's General Presidency, "More Fit for the Kingdom," *Ensign*, April 2009

Sandy immediately recognized that one way for her to both learn the language and serve the people of Ha'afeva was to teach them some of her cooking. During our first district leadership meeting, Sandy spent the day with two of the leaders' wives and taught them how to bake cinnamon bread and cinnamon rings. They were really excited. The next day, a daughter from the house behind us came over and learned how to bake bread, which she did in her umu. Apparently, she was very pleased how it turned out, because she, her mother, and her sick brother ate both loaves before her father came home from the bush. All he got was a good report on the results.

During one district conference, Sandy taught a woman from O'ua how to bake bread. She later came to visit us and was very excited to tell us that she had gone home and baked eight loaves in her umu. We weren't sure what she'd used for pans or how she'd known the bread was done, but it was delicious! She was very proud of herself and said she was going to make cinnamon bread next.

After we arrived in Ha'afeva, Sandy tried out our oven and baked a cake with one of the precious eggs that our neighbor gave us. They must have bragged about it, because when Sandy went to a woman's home the next week to learn to weave, all the woman wanted to do was learn how to make the cake.

After Sandy shared her banana bread made from a short, firm, yellow-orange, blunt-ended plantain or banana called *hopa,* mixed with a little granola breakfast cereal and regular bread dough, people all over the island started asking to learn how to do it. They called it "ma hopa."

We developed a tradition of holding a luncheon with the two counselors in the District Presidency and their wives after our monthly District Presidency meeting. While the men were holding the presidency meeting, the wives were with Sandy learning how to cook American dishes. The wives loved the experience, and it was a good way for Sandy to practice speaking Tongan.

Lupe, one of the wives, later used what she had learned and fooled her friends who cooked things for the National Visitors Center. Lupe said that they should make a special white sauce that she knew how to make that would make the meal at the center much better. She made the sauce or gravy to go over the rice and the people were crazy about the dish. She told them that the people in her village were more advanced than the capital city people who did not yet know how to make such a wonderful sauce. She loved being the country girl with the upper hand.

Two young single adult sisters in our branch wanted to make chocolate chip cookies for family home evening. We agreed, but told them they had to bring the eggs. They agreed but weren't able to find any by late Monday afternoon, so Sandy asked some young kids to go get some. They came back very shortly with five eggs and some kind of exciting story that Sandy didn't really understand. But she was excited to have the eggs, so she rewarded them with some raisins, a new treat for them. A couple of hours later, she began to wonder where they had come up with so many and thought she had better check the eggs to see if they were fresh enough to use. When she cracked one open, there was a developing chick inside. With all the commotion, it hadn't occurred to us that this might be the case. When I questioned the children later, they said, "Yes, the mother had jumped up and squawked a lot when we took them. There are six or seven eggs still there." We explained to them that when they see a lot of eggs together, they should leave them alone. We made the cookies without the eggs, and everyone loved them. We became more cautious of the eggs we received in the future.

One Good Friday happened to also be the eighth birthday for the Branch President's daughter as well as the birthday of Ofa, the little girl next door. Sandy baked a cake for each of them. The Branch President had had mutton, chicken, and hot dogs *koled* (ask a favor) from family and friends in Tongatapu to throw a feast for his daughter. Ofa's family had six children and one more on the way. When we took the cake over to her to sing Happy Birthday, they were just sitting down to dinner. All they had was *ufi*, a plain, potato-like vegetable, and that was it. In the true kindness and charity of Tonga, they offered to share their scanty meal with us. We declined, claiming we were full, and I acted like we'd forgotten something. I quickly went home and got a can of corned beef to add to their meal as a little birthday present for Ofa. These people had almost nothing, but they offered to share it with us. I thought of the other family's feast, and realized what a vast contrast there was, even between people that most Americans would consider poor.

Every week was full of cooking surprises. Things we took for granted were amazing to the villagers, especially the children. One night, as Sandy was preparing macaroni for dinner, Tonga, a little boy from next door, wandered in and wanted to know what it was. He said he had never tasted it. He ate it raw and liked it. He also had never tasted cheese or used a can opener before. After dinner was prepared, the Branch President happened by and stayed to eat. He devoured three huge bowls of macaroni plus several pieces of bread and glasses of lemonade. We had never seen anything like it before. In our displeasure at watching him eat so much, we could see our western culture coming through in not being thankful that we could share with him.

As a young missionary, every house I passed during mealtime would invite us to come and eat with them. We should have been happier to invite him to eat with us.

The next few nights he kept hounding Sandy to make macaroni again so he could have some more. When she did, he brought his wife and child, and when we were finished, he called the neighbor to come and taste it—and the neighbor came, plus his wife and child. There was never a dull moment. We gradually understood the Tongan mindset that being able to share food was a blessing.

We learned from Sandy's home economics how valuable every experience in life can be to you as a senior missionary and that you can use whatever skill or talent you have to make friends and create opportunities for the gospel to be shared. Little did Sandy realize as a young mother that all of the cooking skills she developed would assist her in her missionary work and the development of many treasured friendships.

Our Life on the Sea Was Safe in His Keeping

❖

My trust was in Him who created the seas and defined their bounds. I was on His errand—I knew that I was sent on this mission by the authority He recognizes, and, although the elements raged and the ship swayed and trembled amid the heaving billows, He was at the helm, and my life was safe in His keeping.

President Lorenzo Snow, *Biography and Family Record of Lorenzo Snow*, 49

Because there were so many small islands where missionaries were located, the Tonga Nuku'alofa Mission owned three boats, plus vans for the zone leaders on the larger islands. It was one of the few missions in the world to have its own boats for missionaries to use for travel. In other missions, missionaries travel to islands on local boats, but in Tonga there are no regular boats between many of the islands.

Little did we realize when we received the assignment to serve in Ha'afeva, just how much time we would actually spend on the beautiful South Pacific Ocean. Our time upon the water would create a great love affair with the sea as its magic potions cast their spells upon us and captured us in its net and held us prisoners to this romance. We loved the music of the sea's roar, the unbelievable colors that shimmered over the beautiful coral reefs, and the purity of the fresh sea air. On still, starry nights, our boat seemed to be suspended in space. While we learned that the sea was dangerous, its' frightening storms were never sufficient reason to remain on shore. We knew that the Lord was at the helm and that we were safe in His keeping.

Our Almost Tragic First Boat Trip

Our first trip on the water occurred during the transfer to our first missionary assignment when we flew to Pangai and then took one of the three mission boats to travel from Pangai, Ha'apai to Ha'afeva our new missionary home. Traveling with us was President Malupo, his counselor, two young Elders, and a supervisor from the Church education system. What was normally a two-and-a-half hour boat ride ended up taking us over four hours in a howling storm. This was the first of many boat trips that would be delayed by restless, angry waters, but it was more hazardous than all the others.

As we embarked on our trip to Ha'afeva, the sky started to darken, and shifting winds caused the sea to boil. Our little sixteen-foot boat began to pitch as we rode up each swell, then suddenly rushed down and slammed into the next eight- or ten-foot wave. Each time we slammed into a new wave the hull would shudder with the impact, and the angry waves would regroup for another round. President Malupo was standing up in the middle of the boat, holding on to the roof for dear life to brace himself, when a violent wave with an angry temper crashed against us and swept him into the sea.

My immediate impulse was to jump into the water, but neither I nor President Malupo had a life vest on. The boat was moving away quickly—rough seas don't allow you to stop and turn on a dime, and our helmsman was not experienced and was slow to react. President Malupo was a large man and dressed in a suit, wearing shoes and socks and not able to swim. The sea continued to rage with eight to ten foot waves breaking all around as the storm intensity continued to increase. "The waves were like a pack of hungry wolves, eyeing him and from time to time making a spring at him, almost sure to have him at last." (Henry David Thoreau, *Cape Cod*, Houghton, Mifflin & Co. 1893, 318) At times we lost sight of him as the waves hid him from view as his soaked suit and shoes began to weigh him down.

But President Malupo was being watched over by angels that day. He miraculously kept afloat until we could turn our boat through the giant waves and throw him a life vest. We maneuvered closer to him, but we couldn't pull him into the high end of the boat. We had to circle through the stormy sea again to get the low end of the boat next to him. Finally, I grabbed one of his legs. Others took hold of his other limbs, and straining together we lifted him into the boat. We laid him on one of the benches where he said a silent prayer and rested until he regained his breath.

The tempest was truly raging and the billows were tossing high, and for the president to have survived was truly a miracle. He was a very blessed man. It was a frightening first sea voyage for Sandy and I but we learned these comforting lessons, that the angels had borne him up and that the Lord's promise that the faithful would not perish by the waters (D&C 61: 4–6) had been fulfilled.

Visiting the Branches

We did not have the benefit of being able to travel by car as the District President to visit the branches. Instead we would get in our boat and do business with the branches and it was not unusual to go to three different islands on a single day. We averaged over two boats trips a week to visit members on other islands. We traveled to conduct interviews, deliver messages where there were no phones, attend Branch meetings on Sundays, transfer Elders who served on more than one island, and drop off Church supplies and building maintenance materials. It was almost always an adventure. We often took members of various branches home if we passed by their island on the way to another. We frequently let them off in water up to their waists, and they waded ashore holding their belongings above their heads as we sailed on.

On a typical boat trip, the spray from the waves breaking over the bow soaked us even when the sea was calm. These trips often required three changes of clothes per day: boat travel clothes, missionary attire at our destination, and finally a new set of clothing after we came home and showered. We always carried a small, waterproof duffle bag with us to keep our change of clothing and other items dry.

The tide often determined our plans; some islands were only accessible when the tide was high because of reefs around the islands. Other times, our *eiki vaka*, or boat driver, would have to get out of the boat and walk bare footed across the jagged reef, pushing the boat through the shallows to avoid damaging the outboard motor. Once, on our first visit to an island to deliver an important message, our *eiki vaka* anchored the boat quite a ways off shore because of a low tide. He then dove off the boat, swam to shore, delivered the message, and swam back out to the boat. He was over sixty years old at the time. Sandy and I were struck dumb with amazement our whole way home.

On most of these branch visits, we fished along the way by trolling two or three large handheld fish lines alongside the boat. I was always after the captain to troll when we traveled because we might catch some fish for dinner. On one occasion we caught a Mahi-mahi that was over forty inches long. It was a pretty fish, almost a florescent green with yellow and a white belly. On a few occasions, very, very large fish followed the lines for a while, but they never did strike.

When we got home, we had the Elders clean our fish and cut them up. Then Sandy boiled them. She also boiled some of the root vegetables *ufi, kumala,* or *talo* to augment the meal. When the fish were finished, their eyeballs would turn pure white and be floating around in the water. It was important that they be served with the fish because Tongans love fish heads, including the eyeballs. The Tongans have an interesting way of eating fish. They put the fish, bones and all, in their mouth and eat around the bones—a very noisy process. When they were done they would spit the little bones onto their plates and then suck the bigger bones dry.

We loved going by boat to do business with the members of the branches. If the branches had all been on one island, it would have taken us two or three hours in a car to drive to them to do our business, and return home. With a boat it took all day, but it was wonderful to spend this additional time on the ocean.

Big Boat Travel

Our sixteen-foot boat was fine for travel within our district, but to go greater distances we needed to catch the big inter-island boat, the

Olovaha. The Olovaha was a 125-foot-long, three-deck German-built flat-bottomed boat that tended to bob like a cork in rough seas. To catch it, we had to get up at about one in the morning and go out on our boat to the Olovaha which was anchored about one hundred yards off the reef. On one of our trips to the big boat, we gave a ride to a family of five that was moving to Nuku'alofa. Everything that family owned was packed in two or three suitcases. The boat already had two large empty benzene drums, a big television in a box (which wasn't working, so we were taking it to the PBO to trade it in), an empty propane tank, and our suitcases on board. As we pulled away from shore, we heard a yell. The branch president and his wife and daughter were also going out to the big boat, but the little boat they had intended to ride was overloaded, so we went back and picked them up. I'm not sure how much more it would have taken to overload our boat.

You would need a video to get a real picture of what happened next. Between eight and ten small boats full of people went out in the middle of the night to load and unload supplies, passengers, and other goods that came from Nuku'alofa. They sailed out to the middle of the ocean and waited for the Olovaha to sail up and stop to transact business. When it did, the back of the boat was lowered to a ten-degree angle above the water—just enough so that water wouldn't get into the bowels of the boat. The little boats pulled up to the side of this ramp opening, and people started jumping from the little boats to the Olovaha. Goods were handed to and from the little boats that had just dropped off passengers. Other passengers, whose destinations were in the Lulunga islands, started jumping off the Olovaha on to the little boats. It looked like the little line of ants running to and from their anthill, except these ants were jumping between boats. By two a.m. the Olovaha had unloaded all of its passengers and goods for Ha'afeva and all of the new passengers had embarked.

They didn't sell tickets to get on the boat; you had to pay as you got off. As we entered the boat through the cargo area, which transported everything from livestock to fish, we were often overwhelmed by the stench of engine fumes, vomit, and animal waste. We then went up through very narrow passageways to get to the deck. People were everywhere. There were a couple of stuffy, cramped, claustrophobic indoor rooms you could pay for in advance, and there were benches inside the second deck, but most passengers slept on the open top deck. The outdoor spaces would often be wet, cold, and crowded, but the air was fresh. The toilets were truly awful—overflowing and sloshing around—and the vomiting fellow passengers didn't enhance the experience, either. Though they are a seafaring people, Tongans tend to get seasick as soon as the boat leaves the harbor even if the sea isn't rough.

On this trip, Sandy and I planted ourselves against a wall of the ship, which was about seven feet from the rail. Sandy stretched out to try and get some sleep. When people came by periodically, they just stepped over her and anyone else that was stretched out on the deck. Many people, including me, just stayed awake and talked to friends. On one subsequent voyage Sandy threw her *tupenu* wraparound skirt on the deck and slept next to several ice chests full of fish with her feet next to the head of some man. When I went to sleep I was sharing a bench with an old woman, but when I woke up she was on the floor and I had the bench to myself, which was somewhat embarrassing.

On another trip there wasn't much room left by the time we boarded, so we went up on the top deck next to the captain's area. There was an overhang that I felt would shelter us from the rain that had begun to fall as we started to sail. Sandy was so tired she went right to sleep, but I stayed awake for a while and brushed the water on the deck floor and away from us as best I could. Then I covered my head with my jacket and slept. It stopped raining after a while, and it seemed like it wouldn't be too bad—we were only wet on the parts of our body resting on the floor, while our tops were sheltered by the overhang and our jackets. What we didn't realize when we selected the corner spot was that as the boated tilted with the ocean waves and swells, the water already on the deck would all run from the other end of the boat into our little corner. That night was less like a water bed and more like sleeping directly on water.

Nothing on these big boat trips ever seemed easy or pleasant.

Seeing the Light

One Friday we jumped at the rare opportunity to take the big boat to Pangai to do some "real" shopping for more than the basics we could get from the Ha'afeva stores. We threw some things in a bag just in case we spent the night, and off we went. As we were getting on the boat, there were two *palangi* (Caucasian) men getting off who asked if I was Mr. Banks. When I said yes, they introduced themselves as surveyors coming to survey O'ua for the possible new chapel and tennis court. We hadn't received any notice that they were coming—I guess PBO had just forgotten to call or put the announcement on national radio. Luckily, there was a small boat heading to O'ua, and we got them on it. We went on to Pangai and did our shopping. The big store was already closed, but there was a smaller store that had almost everything we needed. We returned home that same night around 11 p.m.—a typical four or five hours of travelling for one and a half hours of shopping. The most exciting thing we brought home to the members from that trip was a five-gallon box of ice cream.

We were a little nervous as we neared Ha'afeva that night because we couldn't see any signs of the little boats waiting out at sea to pick us up. Neither the island nor the boats had electric lights, so we were looking for waving lanterns. The night was cloudy and pitch black as there were no lights from the heavens lighting up the area. Because we could see nothing, we wondered what would happen if no one were there to pick us up. We asked the captain of the boat, and he told us that he would have to sail on to Tongatapu. We would then have to come back on the next boat, though at no additional cost. The thought of additional 14 or 15 hours on the open deck was not pleasant. As the ship slowed, suddenly a little flashlight flickered up ahead to let the captain know that someone was there. Our nightmare was over. I don't ever remember being so happy to see a flashlight.

While our concern for passage to shore was over, the words of an old favorite Church hymn came into my mind with new feeling and meaning. I remember this experience every time I sing the hymn:

> *Brightly beams our Father's mercy*
> *From his lighthouse evermore,*
> *But to us he gives the keeping*
> *Of the lights along the shore.*
> *Trim your feeble lamp, my brother,*

Some poor sailor, tempest-tossed,
Trying now to make the harbor,
In the darkness may be lost.
Let the lower lights be burning;
Send a gleam across the wave.
Some poor fainting, struggling seaman
You may rescue, you may save.

Hymns, 1985, *Brightly Beams our Father's*
Mercy, no. 335

I thought how members of the Church sit in meetings and sing this and many other hymns dealing with the sea and have no significant feeling for the meaning of the words and their true imagery and symbolism. Elder John H. Groberg reflected my sentiments when he "wondered if anyone could fully appreciate the words and the pleading of these songs until they had been on a 'tempestuous sea.' I sensed that it is probably beyond the grasp of most who have not been in a small boat on a dark night to understand fully the great value of a beacon light on perilous waters. For some reason I felt sorry, not for myself but for those who have never been in a small boat on a stormy sea, where they can feel the truth and beauty of the pleading verse, 'Wondrous sovereign of the sea, Jesus, Savior, pilot me' (Hymns, no. 105)." (Elder John H. Groberg, In the Eye of the Storm, Bookcraft, Inc. 1993, 215)

Shipping Propane

Our stove and refrigerator ran on propane, which we couldn't get on our islands. We had two propane bottles that we alternated using and sending back to Nuku'alofa for a refill. When one was in use, the other was on the boat. Once, the boat returning the propane passed by our island at night, and since they didn't have to drop off or pick up any passengers or other cargo, they delivered the propane bottle by throwing it overboard and letting the waves wash it up. The villagers informed us the next morning that our propane bottle was floating on the reef. It reminded me of how they delivered years ago to the far northern island of Niuafo'ou. They used to toss a large tin can full of mail into the ocean because they couldn't land on the island, and people swam out and retrieved the tin can of mail. The island became known as Tin Can Island. I jokingly wondered if Ha'afeva would now be called Propane Tank Island.

We also had problems getting someone to pick up the empty bottle in Nuku'alofa to get it filled up and returned. It seemed to get lost frequently. To help deal with these delays, we decided to utilize a commercial propane bottle that was over three times larger. When I called the office missionaries and ordered the larger bottle, they told me that they didn't think they had enough time to get it on the boat that day, but they would try. That night we had Siaosi (our young *eiki vaka*) go out on our little boat and meet the big inter-island boat and hopefully pick up the large propane bottle. He was told that there was no large propane bottle on the boat for Elder Banks.

When important things are shipped in the islands, the sender often pays to broadcast a notice of the cargo on the national radio station news. This ensures that there are no secrets in the islands. We hadn't received a notice broadcast that our propane was coming, so the next morning I called PBO instead of the office missionaries and asked them if they could get one large propane bottle on the boat that was leaving that afternoon. They said they would, and we received a broadcast about the shipment on the national radio news that night. Late that afternoon, after all the arrangements were made, I met a young man in town that had been on the boat the night before, and he told me that he had seen a large propane bottle on the ship with my name written on it. But by now it was too late to stop the shipment of the second bottle.

The next day we picked up the bottle that had been sent by the PBO, and, lo and behold, the same boat had the small bottle that we'd sent off two weeks before to be refilled. To our surprise, it was still empty. Somehow it had never been unloaded in Nuku'alofa and had been riding around the boat circuit for two weeks. We took it off and put it in storage. The next night the boat with the large bottle we'd ordered from the mission offices returned to Ha'afeva from the trip north to Vava'u. We retrieved it, satisfied that we now had enough propane to last us for a long time.

Members Sailing

It was overwhelming to see how Church members would sacrifice to attend district conferences. We would sit in our nice house behind the chapel in Ha'afeva and see members walk by soaking wet from their two-hour boat rides. They literally took their lives in their hands when they went out on rough seas, but they not only came, they brought their whole families (one family even brought a little puppy) and all the food they would need for three days of meetings as well as for the huge feast for the president and the other visiting authorities. It was amazing. It reminded me of a Banks family reunion with people sleeping all over the place. The main difference was that these people slept out under trees or even in the open, hoping it wouldn't rain! People stayed up late at night talking like kids at a youth conference. There could be fifteen people sleeping in the one-room missionary house next door. They didn't seem to have much luggage with them, but at the dance on Saturday night and at Church on Sunday morning, the women wore lovely dresses, and the men sported suit coats and freshly ironed white shirts, and we wondered where they came from.

One of the branches performed a ballroom dance for our first district conference. A branch member learned a dance in America which she then taught others and performed for the conference. All the women had lovely white dresses and the men black coats with tails, pants, and black bow ties to go with their freshly pressed white shirts. It was a stark contrast to the Tongan dance the same group had done earlier. We marveled to understand how they had brought these clothes in a boat that dropped off its passengers soaking wet from ocean spray.

The Sea as a Learning Experience

Our adventures on the sea taught us that you need a trusted man at the helm, one who has been tested by the sea, one whose eyes can see beyond the horizon to the distant shore and not be fooled. This trusted individual must be someone who can draw upon the strength and power of his faithful, seagoing Polynesian ancestors and upon his own years of experience and training. He is an individual who knows and understands the location of the reefs and their narrow openings to the shore, and the times of high tide and low. He is someone who marks his course and knows both where he has been and where he is going. Anyone can sail upon the glassy sea, but the trusted helmsman understands that there is a panting tiger beneath it, and that the velvet paws of the surface conceal its remorseless fangs. He is one who has faced those fangs when the seas were raging, when fierce winds beat upon him as he toiled in the howling storm. He has slain the tiger and safely guided his boat to safe harbors.

We learned that these same principles applied to the leadership throughout the Church. While we all know that the Lord is at the helm, we also know that there are various helmsmen throughout the Church providing leadership in many capacities. They too must be trusted because of their experience and vision. These leaders know the path to follow to deliver their fellow passengers past the jagged reefs of spiritual destruction to the safe shore. They know where they are going and where they have been. They are prepared to help their fellow passengers pass through the storms of life and slay the adversary who lurks beneath the surface of so many of today's activities.

We also learned that the promises of the Lord are true. We traveled frequently upon the beautiful and sometime fearful seas and learned from many experiences that the Lord and his angels were watching over us and while there many dangers upon the waters we would not perish if we were faithful,. We trusted in God and knew we were on His errand, that He was at the helm, and our lives were safe in His keeping.

Learning How to Measure the Church

The Brethren recognize that units of the Church are at different stages of development and have different needs . . . The Savior's Church in all dispensations, where it has been established, began simply with a basic organization and basic materials . . . It does not take a complicated Church organization or a full library . . . to help Church members mature in the gospel. What they need . . . is the influence of the Spirit to give divine direction and faithful obedience.

Elder L. Tom Perry, First Worldwide Leadership
Training Meeting, January 2003

When President Malupo called me to be the president of the Lulunga District, he instructed me to prepare Lulunga to become a stake. With the President's instructions in mind, I began diligently searching the handbook of instructions and trying to organize the full Church program. We had come from a well-organized stake and ward, and my initial approach was to implement the full Church program without considering the available leadership or the actual number of members they could serve. It was my goal that by the time we left, they would have their records in good order and would be participating in all the basic programs of the Church, including home teaching and visiting teaching.

What I failed to recognize was that the Church was made for man, not man for the Church. I didn't appreciate many of the practical things that had to be done to achieve my lofty goals. The instructions of President Harold B. Lee that "the programs and activities of the Church, as important as they are, always need to be seen in that overall perspective" would have been helpful to me. He continued, "There are subordinate ways and means of assisting us in reaching these larger goals, but one should never confuse the importance of way stations on our journey with the greater importance of the final destination of our journey. In our attitude about programs and procedures, we must avoid making the error of the Pharisees, who in their thinking thought man was made for the Sabbath. The quorum, for instance, exists to serve men and their families, not the reverse. To paraphrase, man was not made for the Church, but the Church was made for man. Whatever programs we launch must always be measured by our effectiveness in meeting the needs of the individual members . . ." (President Harold B. Lee, *The Teachings of Harold B. Lee,* Deseret Book, 1966, 383)

The members were a smart, humble, and spiritual group, but they were not educated about the complex Church organization and reporting system, and the size of the branch membership's limited the availability of leadership. I was not aware at the time of a January 13, 1923, First Presidency letter which warned: "The work of the Church, in all fields, is standing in grave danger of being regimented down to the minutest detail. The result of that will be that not only will all initiative be crushed out but that all opportunity of the working of the spirit will be eliminated." It took me some time to learn that the spirit among the members was more important than the sophistication of the organization. Over the next ten months, we taught them about sophisticated systems and organization, but they taught us about humility and faith.

Elder John H. Groberg learned fifty years earlier "that substance is more important than form, [and when we learn that,] then we can focus more on things that really make a difference. Using paper and keeping records was not a part of Tongan culture then. The heat, humidity and lack of storage, as well as the cost of pens and paper, made it basically impossible. More than that, however, I wonder if they didn't understand better than we do that substance is much more important than form, and the Spirit always measures substance and justifies action." (Elder John H. Groberg, *In the Eye of the Storm*, Bookcraft, Inc., 1993, 196) This same culture existed in the remote islands of the Lulunga District.

I had a number of discouraging moments during my first weeks as District President. Sandy diagnosed it as Satan working on me. After one conversation with some people that created a great deal of misunderstanding, I was about ready to get on the boat and go home. I had told President Malupo not to make me the District President, but he felt differently. It is difficult enough to lead in your own language, but to do it in a language I struggled with was a great challenge. I continually called upon the Lord for His help and told Him that if He wanted me to do a good job, He'd better bless me with the gift of tongues in the Tongan language. It wasn't exactly a demand, but it was close.

I realized very quickly that this assignment would be the greatest challenge I had ever faced in the Church. I couldn't even call the mission president to get advice because he was always on the road and telephone service was almost nonexistent. They say that no man is an island, but this may have been close to it. Fortunately, I had Sandy to lean on. She was great about the whole thing. I don't think that anyone can understand what a great challenge this assignment was to her. She'd had six weeks of limited practice with the language, yet she had to be with it every day. I, at least, could understand it reasonably well, but she understood nothing most of the time. Some of the Elders spoke some English, but most of the time the people only spoke Tongan. What great faith she had throughout this assignment! This time of truly having to rely on each other helped me better understand the blessing of the companionship of a trusted spouse.

Our first challenge was to visit the O'ua Branch and install a new branch president. (The previous one had been called to be one of my district counselors during district conference.) We left at seven a.m. Sunday morning and went for a thirty-minute boat ride to pick up my other counselor and his wife in Matuku. Then it took us another hour and a half to reach O'ua because the tide was out, forcing us to go around the island the long way to get around the reef. For this trip, however, the sea was not rough, which proved a bit unusual.

When the district presidency visited a branch in the Lulunga District, the meetings started when the visitors had arrived and changed out of their wet clothes. By the time that happened, the members were assembled in the chapel. There was only one problem—I needed to interview the two candidates for counselors in the branch presidency. What a great challenge this was with my weakness in Tongan! The interviews were long, probing, and difficult because of my limited language skills. The interviews took over an hour, and most of the people sat in the chapel or wandered around outside waiting that whole time. It was a far cry from our meetings in North America.

Following the interviews, we held our meetings with the members, which were in turn followed by a big feast before our trip home. It was a little faster coming home because the tide had come in so we could return the shorter way.

District Meetings

It was hard to measure the success of the meetings with the district council and branch presidents. We had the two meet together so that I could do leadership training from the Melchizedeck Priesthood Leadership Handbook. These people were great, but many had not taken the opportunity to study the gospel. Some leaders didn't have copies of all of the standard works, and what they did have they didn't read very often. Most of these people were not raised in the Church, so they had not had a lot of training about gospel principles apart from priesthood and Sunday school lessons. When I instructed them to read Sections 20, 84, and 107 of the Doctrine & Covenants, they were amazed that the answers to their questions could be found there. During frustrating times like this, Sandy often reminded me that I was trying to eat the proverbial elephant in one big bite instead of one bite at a time.

One important thing we developed was some good dialogue among the brethren. They were not used to group discussion form of meeting, but they seemed to catch on pretty fast. In one of the first meetings they came up with some recommendations for a young

adult activity. They also suggested rescheduling the district conference to the middle of the week to allow more nonmembers to attend
and deter members from having to travel on Sunday to return to their
villages.

After each meeting, the unit leaders gathered at our storehouse
to get benzene boat fuel, which the Church provided for the trips to
the district leadership meetings. I had a two-hundred-liter drum of
benzene that we used to fill their containers. This took some time, and
because of the length of the meeting and the time that it took to get
the benzene, they often missed the right tide and had to wait until later
in the day to return to their various islands.

Home Teaching Impacted by a Pig

One thing that we worked on over the first few months was getting
home teaching going.

My father had taught me the importance of home teaching, and I
tried to ensure that this important activity occurred in our district.

To be a good example, I was the companion of one of the older
men in the Ha'afeva Branch. We were assigned three families and we
visited them all the first month. The second month was a different
story. Each village in the Lulunga area has a fence built around it to
keep the pigs and goats from going into the bush and eating peoples'
gardens. Even so, pigs occasionally got through the fence and into
people's produce. It seems that my home teaching companion had
been having a problem with his garden being invaded by pigs. He
wanted to catch the culprits, so he called the police in Pangai to find
out whether he could kill pigs he caught in the bush eating his garden,
and they reportedly told him that he could. That night he went to the
garden and waited for the trespassing pig. Sure enough, it came, and he
beat it to death. Unfortunately, the pig was pregnant at the time, and
evidently it was illegal to kill a pregnant animal, so the owner of the pig
called the police headquarters in Pangai and pressed charges against
my home teaching companion. And it just so happened that the owner
of the pig was one of the people we home taught. It would have been
a little awkward to home teach someone whose expectant pig you had
just killed, so I was forced to change companions.

Using the Priesthood

Tongans in our remote islands had lots of experience while growing up in preparing feasts, planting gardens, and catching fish, but conducting meetings and performing priesthood ordinances were a different thing! One of the issues that we had to deal with early on was the fact that the local Church leaders relied on the full-time missionaries to do all priesthood ordinances. Foni, a Melchizedek Priesthood holder, performed a priesthood ordinance for the first time when he blessed his infant son. When he concluded, I thought about how many priesthood holders had performed ordinances for the first time in Ha'afeva since we'd arrived. Siaosi, one of our eiki vaka and the first counselor in the branch presidency, confirmed his sister a member of the Church, consecrated oil, and assisted with the administering to the sick. Valoa blessed his grandson, and Foni blessed his daughter. None of these men had blessed any of their previous children. Some of these priesthood holders were still very young. In fact, they were younger than the youngest of our children.

Siaosi was often very reluctant to take the lead. He once asked one of the missionaries to give the priesthood lesson, and the missionary declined because I had asked him to. I had hoped that Siaosi would give the lesson, but his solution was not to hold priesthood meeting at all. I had Siaosi meet with me later, and I gave him an outline and taught him how to give a lesson. He gave a very good lesson the next week, and teaching didn't seem to be an issue with him anymore.

I also had to prepare Siaosi to confirm his sister. He'd asked that I do the confirmation, but I told him that it was his responsibility to do the ordinance because she was his sister. After working to prepare him, he did a fine job. Siaosi was a twenty-four-year-old convert to the Church. He had joined when he was a teenager and had attended Liahona High School in Tongatapu for a couple of years, so he had some exposure to the Church outside of Ha'afeva. Still, he had never before had the experience of teaching a class, organizing a meeting, or performing a priesthood ordinance.

We realized over time that we were expecting men like Siaosi to act the same as our own children when they hadn't had the same training.

We had forgotten that they were still young in the Church and in years. Their understanding would come; it would just take time. We spent a lot of time teaching Siaosi how to be a priesthood leader, hoping that it would pay off in the future. Today, over fourteen years later, Siaosi Lavaka is serving as the Lulunga District President.

Complex Reporting for Simple Branches

The PBO in Tongatapu didn't realize how difficult it was to get the annual church reports to them. Boat travel to and from the small islands of Lulunga made receiving, completing and submitting those reports a lengthy process. To this was added the fact that using paper and keeping records was not a part of small island Tongan culture and most leaders had no accounting skills. The heat, humidity and lack of storage, as well as the cost and unavailability of pens and paper made basic record keeping almost impossible and very slow. It took the faithful branch leaders a lot of time to understand and complete these reports after they received them and then returned them to me by small boat.

On one occasion the PBO said that they would send someone on a plane to get the annual reports from the Branch Presidents if the reports didn't come that week. Because our boat was broken we rented a boat from a non-member to visit each branch and collect and help them complete the reports. I wanted to wait to see if PBO would really come on the airplane to Pangai and then rent a boat to tour the various islands to get the reports, but Sandy didn't think that was the right thing to do, so she pointed me down the straight and narrow. It seemed such a frightful waste of the Lord's money to rent a boat and fly someone on an airplane rather than waiting. If we would only put that much effort into saving souls, the work would really move forward.

We were faced with the same issue with all of our district reporting. There seemed to be too much emphasis by the PBO on keeping records and filling out reports when we had so many more important issues that needed our time and attention. Since I was a Certified Public Accountant, I gave far too much attention to the record keeping. Elder Boyd K. Packer expressed a concern about us worrying about the records and forgetting the spirit. "There are many things about living the gospel of Jesus Christ that cannot be measured by that which is counted or charted in records of attendance. We busy ourselves with buildings and budgets and programs and procedures. In so doing, it is possible to overlook the very spirit of the gospel of Jesus Christ." (Elder Boyd K. Packer, "And a Little Child Shall Lead Them," Ensign, May 2012)

Holding Regular and Timely Meetings

It was very hard for many of these small branches to adhere to a timely schedule of regular Sunday meetings. Their numbers were small, and their members frequently travelled to different islands. We worked very hard to get the branches to hold all of their regular and timely meetings on Sunday, but we were not always successful.

On a visit to one branch, the priesthood meeting started with the teacher, branch president, and me, and one other individual came before the meeting was over. When we started Sunday school, there were still quite a few people missing, including one of the counselors to the Branch President. I decided to go find out if these missing members were sick or if they had a particular problem. This was very easy to do since the town was not much larger than a football field.

Were these people ever surprised when they found me at their door! I told them that I had come to check on them because I wanted to know whether it was a physical or a spiritual sickness that was keeping them from being at Church. Some of the families that I visited were just beginning to cook their lunch in the "Tongan microwave," or umu. When they get home from Church it is usually ready and they take the food out and eat. It takes time to prepare and if you don't get up and started you are late for Church.

All of the people that I visited attended Church, including one that I interviewed to be the new first counselor in the branch presidency. In my sacrament meeting talk I addressed their tardiness. I tried to subtly teach them with what I thought was humor in my talk that did not connect with them. I read the parable of the ten virgins from Matthew but read it to them by changing the oil in the lamps to preparing food in their umus, saying that some of the virgins hadn't gotten up on time and their umus were late. They did not view what I was reading as fictitious or humorous. Sandy thought that the story sounded different, but she was still learning Tongan. She knew the correct version. I never did that again. I thought that they might get a kick out of the change. I even tried to explain what I had done after the fact but it didn't seem to register as humor to them. Obviously there are often cultural differences in humor.

On another Sunday visit to one of the branches, the Sunday school and Primary teacher had gone to Pangai to visit family, so there was no one to teach their lessons. Also, no one had prepared the lesson for priesthood meeting. Sandy ended up teaching Primary, I taught the priesthood lesson, and one of the visiting full-time missionaries taught the Sunday School lesson that he had taught in another Branch the previous week. After that, we tried to always be prepared to give the various lessons just in case the teacher was absent.

It was a challenge to teach the members to think ahead about the fact that if they were out of town they wouldn't be able to fulfill their assignments. Unfortunately, most of the traveling members never knew how long they would be gone, and you couldn't phone anyone to find a substitute because the only phones in the district were on Ha'afeva. In spite of all this, there was a good spirit at the meetings, and I believe they enriched everyone.

When we arrived for one branch visit, the branch president told us it was Father's Day, which we didn't know. When it came time for the meeting to start, the branch president said that it was going to start an hour later. The hour passed and it was time to start, but the two missionaries working on the island who had been asked to give the priesthood and Sunday school lessons were both sick, so we just sat for another hour without anyone giving the lesson.

After a while, a woman who said that she was a Primary teacher called all the children to come out and the children stood by a hall wall and sang a few songs. They couldn't go to their classroom to teach them because it was the room in which the sick missionaries were staying. The woman gave a forty-five-second review of a lesson in the hall and then they sang a couple of songs they had prepared for Father's Day, and we all went back in the chapel and waited a little longer for the branch president to come back. Finally, Sacrament meeting started and was over in an hour or so. Their three hours of meetings had been narrowed down to two hours of waiting and one hour of meeting.

We learned that the inability to hold the full slate of regular and timely meetings was a result of the small size of the branches and the lack of discipline and not because of a lack of faith.

Missionary Callings from the District

We had the blessing of assisting two young men with their missionary applications. In early April we spent a lot of time with one of our young men from Ha'afeva getting his missionary papers completed, signed, and submitted. The forms had to be completed in English, so I had to give a little more help than would normally be necessary. At that time, the Church required Tongan missionaries who received Church financial assistance to make a $250 financial contribution with their missionary application. This contribution ensured that the prospective missionary made a significant effort to finance his mission—the Church missionary fund would cover the rest of his expenses. This prospective missionary had planned to go on a mission in January, but he did not have the $250 for his deposit.

We worked with him to get his papers and money in order and mailed, then waited and waited. In late May, President Malupo called me He said that there was a problem with the application but that it would be taken care of. When President Malupo was released in July, I still had not heard anything. I asked President Kivalu, the new Mission President, to look into the situation. He couldn't find any record that the papers had ever been filed, let alone where they were. After much searching, the papers mysteriously turned up on someone's desk. The mission secretary said that he would contact one of his friends in the Missionary Department to get the papers expedited.

August passed, and when the end of September came I asked the missionary secretary the status of the application. He then confessed that it was an error to send them directly to the missionary department in Salt Lake City. They should have been sent to the Area Office in New Zealand, but they had now been sent there. He told me he would check their status. Two days later I got a phone call from the

PBO asking if the missionary had received his call. I told them the young man had not received his call. They then explained that they had just been advised of his call and because of the short period of time before he would go overseas they had to start the visa and passport processing immediately.

This process had started in April and now, in September, we find out something. The PBO requested that the young man come to Tongatapu immediately to start the visa and passport process because he had been called to the Australia Adelaide Mission. I went immediately to his house and found out that he had gone to Tongatapu on the inter-island boat the night before to look into what was happening. He was truly moved by the spirit to go when he did, for he was able to report the next day to the PBO and start the process. His family was very excited about the fact that he was going outside the country. Since Tonga was providing all of its own missionaries few of them currently were sent overseas. Some of the people thought I must have worked some kind of miracle in the way I filled out the forms for him to be able to go on a mission outside the country.

The belief that I could work miracles of getting missionaries called on foreign missions was confirmed in the members' minds when word was received a short time later that the son of my first counselor had been called to go to the New Zealand Wellington Mission. I had now helped prepare the missionary papers of two missionaries from the Lulunga District, and they had both been called on foreign missions. I joked with some of the members that people would start moving into the district so that I could help their sons prepare their missionary forms. Everyone knew, of course, nothing I did dictated where the missionaries would go. These were calls from the Lord through the Prophet.

Culture Differences in Church

We encountered a number of memorable cultural Church experiences during our service in the Lulunga District. The following anecdotes give insight into the kinds of differences that can be experienced by senior missionaries throughout the Church.

During the sustaining of Church officers at the Matuku Branch Conference, a little five-year-old boy raised his hand for a negative vote. We didn't know if it was done mischievously or he just didn't know better, but the leaders took it very seriously. They stopped the meeting and took the small child out of the room to find out his objections. I was impressed that they knew what to do when someone objected, though surprised that they took the boy's action so seriously.

We had a man come to the house one day with seven very large *ufis*, or white yams, to pay his tithing. He was going to Tongatapu the next day and would be gone for a few months, but he wanted to pay his tithing before he left. Our current Church system is not well set up to handle these types of situations where the items have to be sold to convert to cash, but he fulfilled his responsibility.

One of our early Sundays was a missionary farewell where the branch president became very emotional during his talk. Instead of reaching into his pocket and taking out a handkerchief (which most Tongans do not carry), he took his tie and used the back of it to wipe the tears from his face. It was nothing unusual to anyone but us, and I realized later that it was not only standard procedure, but actually very practical.

None of the stores on Ha'afeva or any of the islands in the district sold any bread, so we generally used hard crackers for the sacrament. One week we thought we saw dark bread in the sacrament tray, but when we partook we realized to our surprise that it was actually broken-up gingersnaps. Through it all, we came to realize that though the Church is true wherever you are, there are always cultural differences.

Measuring the Things That Count Most

Too often we measure progress in the Church through numbers, statistics, percentages, and other quantifiables. This was almost impossible in these remote islands of Tonga because we were not able to maintain accurate records. We learned that there are things not so easy to see or count which more accurately measure progress in the Church. I now believe that "far more important than counting the things we can *see* are those spiritual things we can *feel*." (Elder Boyd K. Packer, "The Library of the Lord," *Ensign*, May 1990) It is, however, difficult and almost impossible to measure and weigh spiritual things we can feel by man's yardstick or scales.

I believe that a better way to measure the progress of the Church in the Lulunga District was to review how they demonstrated their love of God and their fellow man. I didn't have a spiritual stethoscope to place on the heart to measure the love that beats in the breast of an individual, but I could see and feel their love for God and his children. The Savior told the people in the meridian of time that all the law and the prophets were the founded upon the principle of unconditional love of God and our fellow man. I found love abounding among these Saints. These people lived simple lives that did not create barriers between them and their God. They had none of the modern idols like TV, movies, and electronic devices to worship. Their love was evident in their long-suffering and kindness. (1 Corinthians 13:4) It could also be measured by their lack of fear. The Book of Mormon tells us, "perfect love casteth out all fear" (Moroni 8:16). The same principle is affirmed in 1 John 4:18, which states, "There is no fear in love; but perfect love casteth out fear: because fear hath torment. He that feareth is not made perfect in love." These people feared nothing and loved much. In doing so, they measured up. These members had within them the pure love of Christ, or charity. While they lacked statistics, reports, and programs, their faith in God was so strong that they were full of charity. With this charity, they were clearly candidates to inherit that "place which thou hast prepared in the mansions of thy Father." (Ether 12:34)

Learning by Study and by Faith

◆

In the Book of Mormon Nephi wrote, "Great are the promises of the Lord unto them who are upon the isles of the sea" (2 Nephi 10:21). One of the promises of God to these people is the gift of faith, which is shown by their simple trust and a certainty that God will provide.

Elder Thomas S. Monson, "Friend to Friend: Talofa Lava," *Friend*, May 1972.

I was troubled because so many of the people in our district did not read the scriptures and other Church materials. I wondered how they learned of the Savior when they did not study His life or His instructions. To encourage the members to read the Book of Mormon, Sandy made up a seminary type chart with the names of members in the Ha'afeva Branch and how many days they had read from the Book of Mormon. When they came by the house they reported on their reading, and the block for that day of reading was marked in red. The length of the red indicated how many days someone had read. However, this only motivated the competitive members. We constantly petitioned the Lord to give us direction in this area.

I searched the Book of Mormon and other scripture trying to understand how the people of those times, who didn't have personal copies of the scriptures, learned the gospel other than by preaching and testifying in the spirit. I knew that King Benjamin did have his memorable sermon at the temple copied and distributed to the people, but that appeared to be unusual. The scriptures were not generally available during the period that Christ preached, but we hear Christ telling the people that they haven't understood the scriptures of the Old Testament. I sought to understand how people during these other periods grew in knowledge and advanced their understanding when they didn't have access to as much scripture as we have today.

Doctrine & Covenants 130:18–19 notes that we will have advantage in the world to come based on how much knowledge we gain in this life. How did the people of those periods develop their knowledge? The people in these remote islands were faced with similar problems, and I wanted them to gain the necessary knowledge to find greater happiness in this life and in the world to come. I knew that the Doctrine & Covenants talked of learning by study and also by faith. But how do you learn by faith? This type of learning seems to require a higher level of spirituality than learning by study.

As I pondered and studied this issue, I read the words of the Lord to the people of Nephi: "Know ye not that I, the Lord your God, have created all men, and that I remember those who are upon the isles of the sea?" (2 Nephi 29:7) And, "Great are the promises of the Lord unto them who are upon the isles of the sea." (2 Nephi 10:21) While I could not find the specific promises the Lord had made to those upon the isles of the sea, I did find an answer in the words of Paul to the Ephesians: "By grace are ye saved through faith; and that not of yourselves: it is the gift of God." (Ephesians. 2:8) Faith is a gift of God, an endowment from on high (1 Corinthians 12:9; Moroni 10:11). Surely one of the promises God granted unto these people of the isles of the sea was the gift of faith to believe in Him and act in His name.

He gave a gift of faith to His children of the isles of the sea like the faith of the children of Israel who transported the Ark of the Covenant under the leadership of Joshua (see Joshua 3:7–17). The Israelites came to the river Jordan and were promised that the waters would part and they would be able to cross over on dry ground. Interestingly, the waters did not part as the children of Israel stood on the banks of the river waiting for something to happen; rather, the soles of their feet were wet before the water parted. The faith of the

Israelites was manifested in the fact that they walked into the water before it parted. As the Israelites moved forward, the water parted, and they crossed over on dry land.

God gave a gift of faith to His children of the isles of the sea like the faith of Nephi when he, with his brothers, was assigned to get the plates from Laban, after two failed attempts was not dissuaded, and "not knowing beforehand the things which I should do. Nevertheless I went forth."(1 Nephi 4:6-7) Nephi went forth on blind faith, stepping into the darkness beyond the light.

God gave a gift of faith to His children of the isles of the sea like the faith of David when he met Goliath. David knew that God was with him. "He will give you into my hands," said the young shepherd boy. And it was his simple faith, his sublime trust, his absolute confidence in the Almighty that overthrew the Giant—not merely a sling with a stone in it.

He gave a gift of faith to His children of the isles of the sea like the faith President Gordon B. Hinckley entreated us to develop, a "simple faith, an unquestioning conviction that the God of Heaven in his power will make all things right and bring to pass his eternal purposes in the lives of his children." (Gordon B. Hinckley, "Faith of the Pioneers," Ensign, July 1984, 6)

He gave a gift of faith to His children of the isles of the sea like the faith of a child, a simple, uncluttered, strong faith unclouded by the philosophies and learning of men, a faith not unduly concerned about the intricacies, the complexities, and the seeming contradictions that trouble many of us, a faith full of unshakable assurance and absolute confidence that God will hear our pleas and grant our petitions. This is a faith we must develop to "become as little children" (Matt 18:3) to allow us to enter into the kingdom of God.

Elder Mathew Cowley speaks of this faith "the islanders have, and that is very simple faith. You know their minds are not all confused with psychology, psychiatry, and all these other things. All they know is just a simple faith in God and his power. They have implicit faith in the fact that they have been preserved down through the centuries. They know, I think, down within themselves, that they are God's children; that they are of the House of Israel. . . . They have accepted God's power as the simplest thing in the world. In the matter of illness, they send for an Elder and have him bless them, and that's that. He represents God, that's all there is to it. As a result they have wonderful manifestations of their simple faith." (Elder Matthew Cowley, *Matthew Cowley Speaks*, Deseret Book, 1954, 147)

While I knew that the people in these islands had great faith, I had a hard time understanding how that faith could transfer knowledge to them. Because I had a lot of education, I had difficulty understanding that anyone could come to a knowledge of truth without having done a significant amount of study. The longer I lived among these people of the isles of the sea, the more I began to understand that people can learn truth through the powerful witness of the Holy Ghost before they learn all the details about the truth through study. Alma preached this when he stated, "And now as I said concerning faith—faith is not to have a perfect knowledge of things; therefore if ye have faith ye hope for things which are not seen, which are true." (Alma 32:21)

Learning by faith is not the transfer of knowledge from a teacher to a student through teaching a lesson. Rather, it is the confirmation of the Holy Ghost that something is true. A fourteen-year-old young man in a small wooded grove in New York did not have significant knowledge by study, but he did have faith that he exercised by kneeling down and praying in those serene woods. That spring in 1820, he gained great knowledge about God the Father and His Son Jesus Christ though faith and not study. I realized that I, too, have learned many things from experiences in my life by exercising faith that I could not have learned by study. As I pondered these things, I came to understand that much of the gospel learning by our members in the district had come through the experiences they'd had with the power of the Holy Ghost.

While many did not gain knowledge by study, there were some individuals that gained great strength from the study of the written word. On one Sabbath trip to Matuku, we had a special spiritual experience with a member who was studying the gospel. Soon after we arrived at Church that day, we learned that a young mother that had recently gone with us to the temple for the first time had experienced a stillbirth the previous Sunday. As soon as Church was over, we went to her house to convey our regrets. When we arrived at her house, she was lying on a bed on the floor with the *Teachings of the Prophet Brigham Young* and all the scriptures in front of her. She was studying. This seems like a very small thing, but it greatly uplifted us. Because so many of the people in the district did not study the scriptures, it gave us a great spiritual boost to see her feasting on the word of God and receiving great relief from the pain and sorrow of having lost a child. As Sandy and I left her to return home, we discussed the great rush of euphoria that we had felt and how it caused our spirits to burn within us. Sandy felt that this sister's recent temple experience had motivated her to make better use of the scriptures.

We understood then that the strong faith of the members in these islands had not only provided them with faith-promoting experiences, but that these same experiences had given them a comprehension of gospel truths. A majority of our members had gained gospel knowledge the same way as Jesus—by the things that He experienced. (Hebrews 5:8)

Blessed are the Children

$$\maltese$$

Let us [n]ever forget the need to respect these, our little ones. Under the revealed word of the Lord, we know they are the children of God as we are children of God, deserving of that respect which comes of knowledge of the eternal principle. In fact, the Lord made it clear that unless we develop in our own lives that purity, that lack of guile, that innocence of evil, we cannot enter into his presence.

Gordon B. Hinckley, *Be Thou an Example*, Deseret Book, 1981, 39.

We learned very early the importance of the children of Ha'afeva in our role as missionaries. We saw that their spontaneous love and laughter would take away much of the humdrum of routine daily living, lend diversity to our lives, and even awaken in us memories of our own childhood and child rearing. Their reveling in the simple exuberance of childhood was our envy. They helped chase away our self-centeredness and selfishness and even changed the direction of our missionary work. No one ever told us what important roles children could play in learning the language or relieving us of homesickness and depression or what the Tongan call *ta'e lata*. Their examples of purity, lack of guile, and innocence showed us how to be more like Christ.

Teaching at the Elementary School

Every Friday morning, public elementary schools throughout Tonga provided a time for each religious denomination to instruct their children in the classroom. Ha'afeva's religious instruction hour began at nine a.m. Before we arrived, the full-time Elders serving in Ha'afeva had taken the responsibility to teach the member children this hour, which continued until a Friday morning when one of the Elders knocked on our door asked us to go teach the class. They had been detained by a phone call and would not be able to go to school. Sandy and I put aside our Book of Mormon translation and threw on our missionary clothes and off we went.

We arrived at the school about ten minutes late to find a room of twenty children waiting for us. We were astounded—there were only four members of the Church at the school. But the instructor for another Church hadn't shown up, so they'd combined those kids with our little group. We sang a few songs and taught them the stories of Lehi and Nephi securing the brass plates and coming to America. After that, we began to regularly teach on Fridays.

Tonga is a religious country, and we were surprised to find that there was little freedom of religious choice in school. We regularly had a few nonmember children come to our religion class, but after our class started a big boy or girl with a stick would come to the window searching for their lost sheep. Usually, the young, frightened nonmember children would slip out and return to their original classes. One class, after teaching a lesson on keeping the commandments, we taught our students the English version of the primary song "Keep the Commandments." As soon as we started teaching an English song, kids began leaving their own religion classes to come to ours. Suddenly a young boy, who served as a kind of sergeant at arms, came with a stick and hit the kids and chased them back to their own class.

It turned out that school discipline in Tonga was much harsher than in western cultures. Beating children with sticks was commonplace. The two boys of our neighbors, Kisi and Akesa, stayed home from school for an entire week while their dad was in Tongatapu. The day before he was due home, a teacher from the elementary school came to their house and beat the boys with a stick for missing too much school. We found the discipline in the schools to be extremely harsh and knew that the teachers would be much more effective using love and praising good behavior.

Sandy always strived to make our lessons hands-on and enjoyable for the children. It became a stimulating experience each week to come up with something new to that would teach them and challenge them. For our lesson on Moses's early life, she made play dough out of flour, salt, and water. When we finished the lesson, we had the kids use it to sculpt things from the story. The kids had never worked with clay or anything like it (except wet sand and mud). They had a great time making baby Moses in the basket, a well, the sheep, and other things from the story. We brought all their creations home to dry and told them that we would return them during next week's lesson. Some of the kids came by the house in groups seeking their little prizes. They were very proud and excited to see their creations drying on our window ledge. The sculptures dried very slowly in Tonga's humidity, so we eventually had to put them in the oven to get them dry. I don't think many of these children had experienced creating something on their own, and we were proud to give them the chance, as it appeared to help their self-esteem.

One week we taught about the Ten Commandments by playing a type of story charades. We told a short story illustrating one of the Ten Commandments and then asked the students to guess which of the commandments it was about. Some of the commandments were hard to describe in story form without giving away the actual answer. It ended up being a fun activity and the class was very attentive. We'd also prepared a connect-the-dots picture of the stone tablets. One of the young boys incorrectly drew the line across the tablet and was brokenhearted when the other kids began to tease him about it. We remedied the situation by telling the class that what he had done was a representation of the stone that was broken when Moses first came down the mountain and saw the golden calf.

We also taught about Abraham offering Isaac as a sacrifice. Sandy created a puzzle from the Church picture files about Abraham offering Isaac as a sacrifice. The picture was pasted on some mat weight paper and cut out using straight lines to form triangles, squares, etc. We timed the students to determine what team could put the puzzle together quickest. They loved competition, and it was a very good learning experience for them. Sandy also created and printed a short fill-in-the-blank test with Abraham and Isaac's story on it. She wrote the words that would complete various sentences on the blackboard. It was very different from America, where the kids complain about taking tests. These kids were excited about the test. In fact, it attracted other students to come and stand outside our little thatched-roof room until we invited them in to complete the questions too. We now had between eight and ten children in our class each week even though we still had the same four members of the Church in the school. No one seemed to chase anyone away from our class with a stick anymore—in fact, the boy that used to chase them away was now coming to our class.

Our best Friday began like any other, but when we arrived at the school, *all* of the school's students were assembled on the front lawn together. This seemed a bit unusual. As we approached, the teachers released all of them—over fifty kids—and they all came swarming up to us. It was only nine a.m., but school was over for the day. We figured that as long as we were there, we might as well take advantage of the opportunity. We had all the students sit down, and we taught them to sing the primary songs "I Am a Child of God," "Teach me to Walk in the Light," and "Keep the Commandments" in English. We had previously made large posters with the English words to these songs that we would take to school each week as well as on visits to branches where we would teach the primary children. We used these posters to teach the entire school. We then played some games with them. Afterwards, a good number of the students walked home with us. We felt like the Pied Pipers of Ha'afeva!

Graduation Parties

Sandy held a big bash for all the girls in the 6th grade at the conclusion of the national exams for matriculation to middle school. It was the talk of the town. Everywhere we went someone asked us about the party. She even printed invitations on the computer so it was really a special thing. You wouldn't believe how excited the young girls were, all eight of them. The national exams lasted two days with four exams each two hours long. At the end of the exams, the families of the kids put on a big feast each of the two days. In America, if we did that, it would be a big thing, but we could always run to the store for the things we had forgotten. Here, they had to plan ahead and call friends and family in Tongatapu to send up boxes of chicken, sheep, etc. on the boat. The kids that pass the exam would go to Pangai or Tongatapu to middle school in January.

Seven of the eight girls invited came to the party and they were very proud to be there. Several of them told Sandy that their mothers or grandmothers told them it was a privilege to be invited to a palangi's home for a party and they should definitely go. One girl wasn't allowed to come and that surprised us because her mother had been quite friendly to us. We found out later that she didn't come because her grandmother, who she lived with, didn't believe she had been invited.

The children had taught us about the Tongan culture; now Sandy would teach them about our culture by fixing a "tea" for the girls. She made bread and some little sandwiches with deviled ham an English couple passing through on yacht trip in the South Pacific left with us. She also baked cinnamon rolls and chocolate chip cookies. She didn't have any eggs, but the cookies still turned out well. She learned to be pretty good at substituting more baking powder and soda instead of eggs. She still had some carrots left with us by someone visiting from Tongatapu so she cut up some of those for the plate. She also made Milo, an Australian hot chocolate, for them and they all sat around the table and ate. It was fun to see them feel so important.

A few days later, several of the 6th grade boys came by to visit. Sandy had mentioned to the girls that maybe we would do something for the boys and I guess they came to see if that was true. They were all jealous that the girls got to have a party so we decided to have one for the boys, also. Needless to say, they were excited, especially when we agreed that we would print out invitations for them, like we had for the girls. Apparently, the invitations were really an important part of the party to them!

Sandy fixed "pigs in a blanket" and catsup, Texas sheet cake, sodas and some little cinnamon pastries and lots of popcorn while they watched movies. They had a great time and we knew that we would miss them when they left in January for middle school. This was another one of those activities that built self-esteem in these young people. We did not look forward to these older boys and girls going away to school, as we had become very friendly with most of them.

Activities with the Children

Because the puzzle for the religion class had been so popular, Sandy decided to make an additional one for use at home. She glued a picture of Christ from the *Friend* magazine on heavy paper and cut it into puzzle pieces of various shapes. We now had two puzzles, and the children—and sometimes the adults—started coming to our home to put them together. A friend from our home ward in Virginia found a couple of small, easy puzzles and shipped them to us. These two puzzles had different pictures, but their pieces were cut to the exact same shapes. We would often mix these two puzzles together and have the kids compete against each other to see who could find and complete one of the puzzles first. They loved doing this. When they'd done the puzzles numerous times, some of them brought their parents over and had a great time beating their parents in puzzle races.

Sandy also made a memory game out of some pictures in a *Friend* magazine. The pieces were tiny—maybe an inch square—but the kids loved it. It became the hottest thing on the island. One morning there were four children at our door by 7:30 a.m., wanting to play the memory game. Occasionally adults would come over to play and kick the kids out. Everywhere we went, we taught the children to sing songs in English and play simple games. They loved it. We always started and closed our activities singing "We're All Together Again," and they soon had it down pretty well. They would come running up to us, wanting to play games and sing, as we were just walking down the street. So sometimes we marched down the main road in a long line singing "We're All Together Again" over and over. Sometimes we'd even sing it while marching around the Church building.

On one of our trips to Tongatapu, the missionary secretary gave us ten little classic reading books such as *Peter Rabbit* and *The Little Red Hen*. She had found them in a closet, and they appeared to have never been touched. The children and the adults that came to our house loved them. I orally translated most of the stories into Tongan so that our guests understood what the books were about. The older kids got a chance to practice reading English with the books, and they gradually began to read or tell the stories to the smaller children.

One of the most useful things we brought with us on our mission was a large box of wooden matches. We used them to light our propane stove and play games like pickup sticks and snatch matches during family home evenings or visits to branches. We couldn't get any new matches in Tonga, so we saved quite a few of the used ones for the games and became quite adept at lighting the stove with a lighter.

One of the great things that we did was to set up a nail game where you simultaneously suspend six nails on the head of one nail without any of the suspended nails touching anything else. I made a small board with a nail in it that we took to all of the conferences to play with and which we played with at home. We always gave them a hint that you construct the roof for a grass house and then put this nail roof on the head of the nail but they would never find the answer so we showed them. After they found out how to do it kids and adults sat around and did it over and over again. You can't believe how much mileage we got out of this game. We also used it as a teaching aide to teach the members that when they think that things can't be done there is always a way if you keep working and thinking about it long enough. This is especially true, if you seek the help of the Lord to show you how.

During all of our time with the children they were helping us with Tongan language and culture. They taught us in a non-threatening manner that made the learning easier, and it made them feel very good about themselves to be able to teach palangi adults. It was another self-esteem experience for them.

Things We Learned About Ha'afeva Children

The children usually came to Church early all brushed and clean. They were very good at sitting still with no books to read, no cheerios to eat, and no paper to draw on. Of course, they did occasionally get up and walk out for a while, but then they would come back in and sit. For the most part the babies were content to sit on the adults' laps. They were all much more sedate than American children, possibly because they're not so stimulated. On the other hand, they didn't have many formal learning experiences.

The people tried to keep their children clean, but many of them would get incredibly dirty during the day. One little boy that came to our house was the personification of the Peanuts character Pigpen. He was the dirtiest little kid in Ha'afeva. He usually looked like he had just rolled in some mud. Once in a while he would come directly to our house after his shower, and it was hard to tell that it was the same little boy, but usually he would bathe and be dirty again two minutes later. The kids teased him about this a lot. He was about four years old, and he came to our house all the time, even though he knew that we would turn him away if he wasn't reasonably clean. We expected all the children to have clean hands if they wanted to read the books and play with the puzzles. Eventually the little boy started coming to our house clean all the time. It was amazing to see. He was also a troublemaker, and we sent him outside several times as a result. After a while he started behaving himself and even insisted that the other children use please and thank you. He loved it when he got to monitor the books and hand them out.

During the process of his reformation, he came one day with very dirty hands. We asked him to go wash them so that he could come in. He left without complaint, but the little girls in the house immediately started carrying on about how he had probably just gone around the corner of the house, to pee on his hands and dry them off before returning. If that's what he did, it was a practical solution, but not exactly what we wanted!

We were never sure when the little boys started wearing underwear. They mostly wore *tupenus*, small skirt-like coverings, and sometimes when they were playing it was obvious that they weren't wearing any underwear. In the Lulunga District, most little boys ran around without pants on until they were two or three years old. This posed a problem when they came to the house. We eventually got quite used to seeing boys pull off their pants to wipe up the wet spot they'd just made on our floor.

One afternoon, we were standing outside a member's home when their three-year-old boy woke up from his nap. We knew he was awake because all of a sudden there was a stream of urine coming out the front door, over the steps, and onto the sand. He followed in a moment, stark naked. Since potty training wasn't necessary on small islands, it made life much cheaper to not buy diapers.

We were visiting Kisi and Akesa next door one time when the kids had just finished taking their showers. They were dressing when we arrived and they just hung a sheet up in the middle of the one room house for a curtain to hide and continue dressing. Their clothes were all in a large wooden chest and they put on whatever they grabbed from the box. If they are younger, they often wear clothes that are quite large for them and the oldest girl often wears clothes that are quite large for her that her mother or friends have outgrown. The box reminded us of the costume box in our home that our grandchildren now use. One advantage in Tonga was that the children all wore uniforms to school. The girls wore red jumpers or skirts and white blouses and the boys wore light brown shorts and white shirts. This did cut down on the number of clothes they had to have but it also demonstrated their poverty level.

While we did not teach the missionary lessons to any of the young children that came to our house, one ten-year-old boy that spent a lot of time putting together puzzles and reading books at our house was baptized. He was related to and referred to as Valoa the younger after our older boat captain. Valoa the elder had mentioned several times that this young man should be baptized, and one morning he asked his parents for permission, brought him to Church, and had him baptized right after the meeting. Very little missionary instruction was given before the baptism, so we sent Valoa the younger to spend some time with the young missionaries. He was the youngest of ten children and had several brothers who had also been baptized, but only one that was still active. This brother had served as a missionary. He had worked for the Church's Liahona High School on Tongatapu for a while but had since moved to New Zealand. Hopefully, this little boy remained active and followed the lead of his older brother. We told Valoa that he was responsible for keeping Valoa the younger active.

While we learned from the children, we also realized the importance of our efforts with them. Although buildings crumble with age and the flowers of spring fade and disappear, the soul of a child is eternal, and any love and help we gave in shaping their personalities was really an investment in the eternities. We realized that the future of the Church in these islands would march forward on the feet of these young children. Our time with the children in Ha'afeva and the Lulunga District was a precious experience that helped us better understand Jesus's words, "suffer little children to come unto me for such is the kingdom of heaven." (Matthew 19:14)

Bob and Alice and the Meaning of Service

❖

For behold, it is not meet that I should command in all things . . . [but] men should be anxiously engaged in a good cause, and do many things of their own free will, and bring to pass much righteousness.

Doctrine & Covenants 58:26-27

Doctor Robert Skankey and his wife Alice were two individuals that took to heart the directive of the Lord to be anxiously engaged in a good cause. They came to Ha'afeva at our invitation to visit and give medical exams to the people in the Lulunga district. They were members of the Church from Ojai, California, and they had been in Nuku'alofa since November of 1997 working with the doctors at the main Tongan hospital. Dr. Skankey was part of Deseret Tonga, a subdivision of Deseret International, a loose network of doctors who would go to various countries at their own expense and help with a variety of medical issues. Dr. Skankey was a practicing OBGYN before he retired. He had previously gone to Bolivia for several months to provide medical assistance to people in isolated areas. Alice was somewhat weak and shaky from Parkinson's disease, but she was a real trooper who didn't want to be pampered, as well as an avid genealogist. While Dr. Skankey was helping the hospital in Nuku'alofa, she was busy working in the genealogy library.

We thought that it would benefit the missionary work in the

Lulunga District to have them come and work with the local Lulunga area "doctor," who was really only a physician's assistant. The real doctors in Nuku'alofa referred to him as a "medical officer." We also wanted to give the Skankeys a little more insight into the old cultural aspects of the country.

They flew to Pangai, the main community in the Ha'apai Islands, where we met them and then took them in the mission boat to Ha'afeva. The Pangai airstrip runs the entire width of the island—literally shore to shore. It also crossed the main road which has gates at each side of the runway to keep the vehicles off when an aircraft is taking off or landing. Even though the runway is fenced, pigs, dogs, and chickens still have to be cleared off occasionally before a plane can use it.

Dr. Skankey and his wife didn't appear to have a problem with our boat trip to Ha'afeva—they were experienced sailors who had owned boats, and Alice had grown up on the sea. However, the Skankeys view of their trip was not the same as ours. To us, the ocean was very calm—it took us less than two hours to travel back. But they had not made the journey on the normal spunky sea between Pangai and Ha'afeva. They described their trip and first impressions of Ha'afeva to their friends and family as follows: "They loaded us onto the Church's boat and away we went for a two-hour bumpy cruise to Ha'afeva. We arrived with a wet bottom along with the windward side of our bodies. My stomach was a little queasy. Both of our bottoms were sore as a result of hard seats. This was really like stepping back in time. About three hundred people live on this island in houses flimsily made of wood, corrugated tin, or thatch. Inside the door less houses is most often one room divided by curtains. The floor is covered by mats, and there is no need for tables or chairs as they eat without utensils sitting on the floor. They sleep on beds or most often on soft mats. It is a land of cooking outdoors over an open fire, a land of fat pigs, [many] skinny dogs, noisy roosters, and chickens. The animals all roam free except on the grounds of the LDS Church. It is well fenced in and is somewhat of a refuge therefore."

We hit the ground running after we landed in Ha'afeva. Dr. Skankey and I went immediately to the medical officer, whom we had previously informed of the Dr. Skankey's pending visit. Dr. Skankey visited the hospital and reviewed the pending cases and available medicines. Dr. Skankey described his visit to the medical officer as follows: "Our first visit was to Viliami the medical officer in his two-bed hospital. It was really trashy before but had become, miraculously, reasonably clean and organized when we arrived. The Banks had told him that a Specialist MD was arriving from the States to spend a day or two with him, and so he had made an attempt at getting the place in order. While Alice started recording genealogies I spent a full day with Viliami seeing patients and discussing therapy. The villagers did not see him in too good of light as he was often drunk and not always responsive to their needs. I explained to each patient what good knowledge Viliami had and how good a "doctor" he was [when he wanted to be]. I hoped that this might stop the cycle of distrust on their part and laziness on his part. It probably won't work but was a good try anyway. His stethoscope was broken, and he wanted me to get him a new one. I told him I would if he would take four evenings of Missionary Lessons from the Banks. I figured that we shouldn't count anyone out, and at least he would know what Mormonism was all about."

Meanwhile, Alice and Sandy went to the elementary school to see the principal and find out when she wanted Dr. Skankey to come and instruct the children on health issues. After the inspection, Dr. Skankey and I went to visit a couple of people in the village that had requested house calls. As we returned from the first house, people started coming to the doctor and telling him of various ailments, from bad backs to a nearly dislocated elbow.

Since Alice was a skilled genealogist, we arrived at a plan that required each person who was examined by Dr. Skankey to fill out a family group sheet and a pedigree chart. This was a very unusual request, but it was received well by the people. Alice and Sandy waited outside with the people and helped them complete their genealogy, Sandy serving as an interpreter.

Dr. Skankey described our visit to the elementary school the next day as follows: "Our biggest thrill in Ha'afeva (as well as the other five islands we visited) was visiting the grade schools. We have much video to demonstrate these experiences. The teachers were all prepared, as we had pre-scheduled our visits. Elder Banks did the interpreting. Alice would give a demonstration of how and when to brush one's teeth, then distributed [to] each a florescent-colored child's toothbrush and a tube of toothpaste. They all then demonstrated their tooth-brushing abilities. It was really cute. They were entranced. I then got up and with my best Cub-master technique told about Germs that were everywhere. When too many of them got on our skin they caused sores and abscesses. There were always a few who had some to come to the front to show off their sores. We told them they could kill germs by washing with soap and water every day. I drew a mean looking streptococci (with legs) on the board and "washed" him with soap and water, and he was erased. The best demonstration I used was when we I used some sausage-shaped balloons we brought. It had a mean face painted on it and was our Germ. When I washed it, I let it go and it flew around the room until it disappeared, out of air. That would get a roar from the kids. We distributed bars of antiseptic soap to each child. We then had them sing and dance for us. What a treat that was. That day in Ha'afeva we taught 52 children."

We had some traditional Tongan food prepared for dinner, including some ufi and manioke along with some fresh fish. The Skankeys had not had many opportunities to eat these things on the main island.

Delivery of a Baby

The night before the Skankeys arrived was the night when the interisland boat came. One of our members, a pregnant woman, had come from the island of Tu'unga to catch the inter-island boat to Nuku'alofa, where she could deliver her baby in a hospital. This was common in our district; most women didn't have any confidence in their local medical officers. When she arrived in Ha'afeva to catch the boat, she heard that there was an American doctor coming the following day. She decided to remain in Ha'afeva and have the palangi doctor deliver the baby.

Early Thursday morning, while we were eating breakfast, this pregnant sister came to the house and asked for a priesthood blessing because she felt like she would deliver the baby soon. We were not all dressed, so I took her next door to the living quarters of the full-time Elders, and we gave her a blessing. Later that morning, Dr. Skankey went to the clinic to see patients with Viliami, and she showed up in labor while they were there. They determined that she was too far progressed to send on a two-hour boat ride to Pangai, so Dr. Skankey sent for Alice and Sandy to come and bring blankets and hot water (the clinic did not have running water). They heated the water in a large teakettle on our gas stove and took blankets from our bedding to the hospital. When Alice and Sandy arrived in the hospital, they realized there was only one piece of linen on the "bed"—really a table—so they had me run home to get more sheets. The supplies in the clinic were minimal to say the least.

Alice and Sandy kept track of the duration and time between contractions while Dr. Skankey continued to see patients with Viliami in the other room. Even though there was no door between the two rooms and there was a window to the outside that would let anyone look in, but the townspeople allowed the mother-to-be her privacy. When delivery appeared to be close, Sandy and Alice told Dr. Skankey to come in and check. By the time I got back with more sheets, we had a new baby girl. Dr. Skankey later recounted, "With the two ladies holding the patient's legs during pushing, we soon had a well-controlled delivery of an average-sized baby girl over an intact perineum. The mother had already had tears or cuts and stitches with her previous deliveries and was pleased to avoid that. The placenta got trapped and had to be manually removed but was not much of a problem. Everybody involved was thrilled, and it was a joyous experience." The mother was excited because the doctor had been able to deliver the baby without any cuts or tears, and because we lifted up her head she was able to watch herself deliver for the first time. This was not the type of missionary experience we expected.

Dr. Skankey had made the delivery a teaching experience for Viliami, who was involved as much as he wanted to be. Perhaps it was all too much for him—the next time they were to get together he disappeared for three days, telling people he was going to visit his wife on a nearby Island.

The grandmother and her sister, as was traditional, named the baby. They chose Alice Roberta after Alice and Robert Skankey so that their service would always be remembered by the child and her family. Like Helaman in the Book of Mormon, they desired "that when you remember your names ye may remember them; and when ye remember them ye may remember their works; and when ye remember their works ye may know . . . that they were good." (Helaman 5:6)

The mother and baby remained at the hospital for a few days, and the four of us visited them daily while we were there. Alice even helped her with some breast-feeding problems as well. When the Skankeys left Ha'afeva, the family presented Alice with a beautiful tapa cloth to adorn a wall of their home.

Visiting the Other Islands

For the next four days we traveled by boat to five different islands. Our first stop was Kotu, a village of about two hundred people. This was about an hour's boat ride through an area spotted with dangerous reefs. One has to be quite experienced in navigating this area to avoid being stranded far from shore on a sinking boat. The Church boats had lost a lot of propellers in this area over the years. Like all the islands we visited, there was no wharf to dock at, so the landing involved either being carried to shore on someone's back through shallow water or jumping into shallow water and wading ashore. Unlike most islands, where the village is on the seashore, you get to Kotu by walking through the bush for about a hundred yards. It is one of the cleaner villages. Flowers often line the main path. It still had its share of pigs, but they were kept from flowers by low fences.

We planned to visit the elementary school on each island to give health instruction and hand out toothbrushes, toothpaste, and soap, as well as tend to various medical patients. This first school was a simple two-room unit with kids sitting on the floor. One patient we saw was sitting on mats under a tarp. The village had one old folding chair, which was the seat of honor for the doctor. We always took our shoes off when entering these homes. Like in all the district's villages, pigs, chickens, and dogs roamed around but would never try walking on mats for fear of a hurled rock. In each village, while Dr. Skankey and I saw to the patients, Alice and Sandy collected completed family group sheets and pedigree charts as payment. As we left one family's dwelling, Dr. Skankey looked down the path and saw a minister in black tails strolling down the lane with his hands behind him. He commented that it reminded him of something out of long ago in the Deep South. Most of the ministers of the various Churches in Tonga wear the long black tail jackets as their ministerial robes.

In the afternoon we waded out in the ocean and boarded our boat to travel to the second nearby island, Matuku. Its' population was slightly less than Kotu's, but the children were just as enthusiastic about our teaching and singing. Their schoolhouse sits on a bluff with a nice view of the ocean. Dr. Skankey described the conclusion of the second island visit thus: "Before we left, they fed us a nice Tongan meal of *manioke, ufi,* cooked plantain, and canned corned beef. They also served a drink of crushed mango, coconut meat, sugar, and water. The Tongans refer to this as *otai mango.* Unfortunately, they used Tongan water from a cistern not palangi water [bottled water] so we could drink only a little. They stand behind us as we eat; when we are finished then they sit down and eat what is left. They also have a trick of eating with their fingers and having a clean hand when they finished. It's remarkable. Whenever I tried it my fingers were gooey and sticky. Perhaps it's because I'm a little hesitant to lick my fingers when through." On our way home, the *eiki vaka* trolled with a plug, as he often did when we were on the water. This time we caught four fish—two bonito and two large fish called *lupo. Lupo* is a favorite of the Tongans because it has a thick layer of fat under the skin. We had Akesa, our next door neighbor, cook the fish into a tasty fish dinner.

The next day we boated two hours to Nomuka, the largest and furthest south of the five islands we visited. There were over five hundred people on this island, which had its own two-bed hospital with a medical officer (a nurse practitioner) who had a public health nurse assigned to her. They both were quite good. They had the respect of the people and appeared to serve the people of that area well. They deliver about 15 babies a year. They were happy to have Dr. Skankey spend part of a day with them, and they saw a number of patients together. We also taught our usual instruction in the local elementary school.

As expected, the members prepared a traditional Tongan meal for us. This is how Dr. Skankey described it: "They had a fine meal for us, which included the usual plus a real delicacy, dried octopus (ugh). It was chewy and fishy. Great stuff if you like it. I think they must call ahead to each island and say feed them diet "B," because each meal was exactly the same as the previous day." After the meal we took our two-hour boat trip back to Ha'afeva to spend the night.

We finished our excursions with visits to the islands of O'ua and Tungua, each a half-day visit doing the same activities at the local elementary school, examining patients, and doing genealogy. While our activities on each island were somewhat repetitious, each group of children was very special and very loveable. We were received with kindness at every turn. The headmaster at O'ua choked back tears as he expressed, in English, his appreciation for helping his children improve their lives.

The process of translating for Dr. Skankey helped me become quite the diagnostician. The patient would tell me where they hurt, and I would translate this to Dr. Skankey, who would then tell me what the patient should do. The patient and I would usually talk for quite some time before the short translation came in English. Dr. Skankey viewed the translation this way: "Elder Banks was the interpreter and got a big kick out of practicing medicine. I would give a treatment plan in one sentence, and he would take ten minutes, elaborating with many gestures and causing much laughter. He was always upbeat and seemed to be very happy in whatever he did or said."

As we took the Skankeys back to Pangai to catch their plane, we reflected on how much we had learned from them about the health problems that existed in Tonga. Almost every woman that came to see the Doctor had a complaint about her back. This occurred because of the many hours they spent hunched over while weaving compounded with obesity. There is also a lot of sugar diabetes and high blood pressure from eating too much fat and salt. It was a great learning experience, and by meeting new people we made it easier for the young Elders to drop in and visit them. Our trip to Pangai was pretty rough, but we did catch a thirty-pound tuna.

The Skankeys came into our lives and quickly left, but they awakened in us a new understanding of the meaning of service to our fellowmen. They were people that made the sky more beautiful to gaze upon. They left footprints on our hearts, and we will never be the same. I believe, like Elder Neal A. Maxwell, that these intertwinings "are not simply a function of mortality but went on before in our first estate, and surely they will continue in our third and final estate! If this is true, what seem to be friendships of initiation here are actually friendships of resumption." (Elder Neal A. Maxwell, *One More Strain of Praise*, Bookcraft, Inc., 1999, 107–108)

Custom and Culture

In addition to the spiritual highlights in the history of the Tongan Saints, there is also much of local color and cultural flavor. Some of this flavor may be subtle, but it increases our delight in the stories and sharpens our vision of what is [Tongan] . . . colored with cultural overtones [they] make each history more readable, more human, and more Tongan.

Eric B. Shumway, *Tongan Saints, Legacy of Faith*, The Institute for Polynesian Studies, 1991, 14–15

All missionaries quickly notice the cultural differences between their mission areas and their homes. They tend to stand out, especially in correspondence with family and friends. Sandy and I were no different. I have high-lighted in this section a few of the unusual customs that caught our attention to illustrate the types of cultural issues that senior missionaries may come in contact with as they serve in areas throughout the world.

Though Tonga's main islands have become more westernized, Ha'afeva is so remote that its mores hadn't changed much from the older traditional customs of the country. The differences stood out even more and provided us with a unique learning experience. Elder John H. Groberg eloquently explained these changes when he said, "It was often sad and sometimes painful to see many aspects of a centuries-old culture swallowed up by a more powerful one led by advanced technology, new ideas, and different ways of doing things, a culture that seemed to roughshod over seas, storms, rain, dankness, and sometimes even people's feelings. . . . No matter what the new technology brought, the need for faith and kindness would never be outmoded." (Elder John H. Groberg, *In the Eye of the Storm*, Bookcraft Inc., 1993, 228)

We learned quickly how culture affected every aspect of the people's lives and realized that the same was true of our own lives. Some of these cultural norms were very different from what we were accustomed. One afternoon soon after our arrival in Ha'afeva, we visited with the mayor or *'ofisa kolo* of the town and his family to introduce ourselves and give them a copy of the Book of Mormon. His wife (who we at first thought was his sister) was out in the yard, cracking nuts into a big bowl. She told us that sometimes the nuts are used to make a soap that's wonderful for cleaning the body. When we showed some interest, she said she would make us some. The next thing we knew the mayor's wife, while visiting with us, was shoving these nuts into her mouth and chewing them. We thought it was quite impolite of her to be filling her mouth so full and refusing to give any to her son or to us. Then she spit all the nuts she'd been chewing into a leaf, neatly wrapped it up, and had her little boy bring it over to Sandy. The chewed nuts were a little ball of soap, and the leaves made it fragrant. Even more surprising, when Sandy tried it later, it worked well.

One unusual custom was related to mothers whose children had lice in their hair. While Sandy was visiting the weaving house, she saw a mother combing her daughter's hair and picking out the lice. When she found one, she picked it out of the child's hair and then put it in her mouth, biting it in half and continued picking out lice. It is certainly a lot cheaper and less work than that NITS stuff. It was later we learned that the lice aren't swallowed but spit out.

Tongans love ice cream, but the way they eat it is a bit unusual. Every time we would go to Pangai, we'd buy ice cream for the Elders and whoever else was there with us that day. With the ice cream we'd buy several loaves of bread. The bread was baked with a division in the middle so that it was easy to break in half. Each person would take a half loaf of bread, hollow out the center, and fill it up with ice cream.

It was actually much easier to eat than an ice cream cone—the Tongan sun melts ice cream very quickly, and without the bread, it would have been running down our arms. They even used these Tongan bread cones with soft drinks.

We also learned a few new cultural tips for homemaking. When you have a big dinner and don't have enough plates it's no problem. Just have the first group eat and then let the next group eat using the same plates. No utensils are necessary and you do the same with the drinking glasses. We learned that plates are not really necessary as we ate off the main plate using our fingers. This way you don't even need to wash dishes. We learned that you can save a lot on paper goods if you do not provide napkins for the dinner guests and just pass around a bowl of water and a towel when the dinner is over. Many of these customs make life more practical and less expensive.

People usually called out for you instead of knocking on your door. We were studying one morning when we heard rocks being thrown on the roof of our house. At first we weren't quite sure what was hitting the roof. We thought it was some of the kids that we had around the house all the time peeking in the windows. They always wanted us to come out and play with them. I was about to go outside and chase them away but Sandy made me sit down and went out by herself. What a surprise it was to find the Siliote our back neighbor, throwing rocks on our roof to get our attention. She had four eggs and some fruit that she wanted to give to us. She was a less active member and with the eggs was giving us something worth the price of gold. She told us one way that the Tongans get your attention when you are in the house is to throw something on your roof so you will come out. When I was in Tonga the first time they didn't have tin roofs only thatched ones so this was new to me.

We learned that the old Tongan culture was filled with beliefs and myths and legends about spirits and ghosts which affected their views in many areas. A couple of the girls told us one night that one of the children in the branch had been hurt by the ghost of Mele Mamonga. She was said to be the ghost of a young Mormon woman who had drowned with her two young daughters while returning to Ha'afeva from a district conference in December 1985. They said she periodically shows up and does bad things, and around Christmas the ocean glows where the boat went down. We had previously heard stories about the drowning—the captain was apparently drunk and showing off by steering with his feet when they hit a wave wrong and capsized. These stories, of course, have grown in the telling.

We wondered why we hadn't seen Akesa our returned missionary neighbor, who attended the Church of Tonga, out visiting with her neighbors and going places after the recent birth of her sixth child. She told us that in the Church of Tonga, women are encouraged to stay at home after giving birth until the baby can be baptized—at about a month old. When she first told us this, we jokingly asked if she was going to stay in her house for eight years. She looked at us like we were crazy or mixed up until she remembered that in our Church we baptize at age eight. She laughed, and we reminded her that we hadn't given up on bringing her family back to the Church. In fact, we told her that we still remembered her family in our prayers morning and night.

One cultural item we learned occurred when we were starting to do square dancing one night. A new young adult woman came and started to do the dance and then stopped and left. She explained that it was *tapu*, or forbidden, to dance with a cousin, and that all the guys there were cousins, so she had to leave. After watching the dance, however, she realized that in dancing "Oh Johnny" you keep changing partners and that maybe it would be all right. An interesting reason, but it makes it tough as almost everyone on these islands is related somehow!

Tongan Borrowing (Kole)

The Tongan word kole means "to ask for a favor or borrow." It was very commonly used with the sense of, "I won't pay you back or return the item unless I happen to remember it or unless you need the same thing some other time." When someone borrowed something we learned to be careful to make it clear if we expected it to be returned. As non-Tongans, we had a hard time getting used to this idea, and we had a hard time believing that it was right for them to be this way. The sharing attitude was wonderful but the taking without asking seemed to be the wrong way. (See Elder Richard G. Scott, "Removing Barriers to Happiness," Ensign, May 1998)

Tongans in the remote islands would often prepare you for a *kole* request by making you indebted to them. We learned very early in our work that when someone from another Church gave us something it was because they anticipated asking something of you. Once the financial minister of the Church of Tonga came to our house with an entire stalk of bananas, and I knew something was up—he had only given us two bananas when we'd given his granddaughter some antibacterial soap. Then, after a little small talk, he pulled fifteen dollars from his pocket to repay us for the benzene that he'd borrowed a few weeks before. He was about to ask for something big.

Sure enough, the kole was to take our Church boat to Pangai so he could catch a plane to Tongatapu. Apparently he'd missed one of the inter-island boats, and unless he got to Pangai it would be almost four days before he could get to Tongatapu. He needed to take the $13,000 raised at his Church's fundraiser and a few other items to their Tongatapu headquarters. Neither his church nor any of its members had a boat, but it was against Church policy to rent the boat, and neither I nor the young missionaries were going to Pangai. We had a problem. I told him to ask the other Churches for the use of their boats and let me know within the hour if they were able. If not, I would call the mission president. It turned out that the reason they wanted to use our boat because it was much faster than any other boat and had more protection from the water so that passengers didn't get wet—they wanted a nice ride, not just any ride. He eventually found another boat, but he had prepared me for his kole very shrewdly.

When Dr. Skankey and Alice attended Church with our Ha'afeva branch we had a lesson in Primary on Choose the Right (CTR), which Alice attended. When Alice got back to Nuku'alofa she bought seven CTR rings and sent them to us for the children in the class. The kids were *very* excited about having their own rings, but later in the afternoon we saw that the kids next door weren't wearing their rings. We found out that their mom was wearing two of them and the other two had been given to two aunts who were visiting from Tongatapu for a funeral. The aunts had made a kole for the rings, so the mother had given the rings to them. While it was hard for us palangi to understand, the children readily accepted the tradition.

Keeping the Sabbath Day Holy

Elder John H. Groberg addressed Tonga's keeping of the Sabbath day in a general conference talk stating: "When Sunday dawns on the kingdom of Tonga, a transformation takes place. If one goes downtown, he sees deserted streets—no taxis or buses or crowds of people. All the stores, all the markets, all the movie theaters, all the offices are closed. No planes fly, no ships come in or out, no commerce takes place. No games are played. The people go to Church. Tonga is remembering to keep the Sabbath day holy." (Elder John H. Groberg, The Power of Keeping the Sabbath Day Holy, *Ensign*, Nov. 1984)

We can learn a lot about Sabbath observance from the Tongan people. While Tonga was not originally a Christian nation, when they did accept Christianity, they made a full commitment to Sabbath observance. Commercial boats and airplanes do not run on Sunday, and banks are not allowed to open. The most famous story of their strict observance revolves around a visit by Queen Elizabeth of England to Tonga. She'd planned to arrive in port on Sunday, but Tonga's Queen Salote informed them that the harbor was closed on Sunday, and they would have to wait until Monday to dock.

I had my own unexpected experience with the Tongan Sabbath. There were no banks on the Lulunga Islands, and none of the stores there would accept checks, so on trips to Pangai, I would cash checks at the Bank of Tonga. On one particular trip, I had a number of checks to be cashed, but the teller wouldn't cash one of them because it had been dated as Sunday. The law mandated that not only would banks close on the Sabbath, but that checks written on that day were invalid. I suggested putting the number "1" in front of the figure to make it a different day. The teller was not amused. She said that if the date were changed, both of the signatories of the check would have to initial it. I ended up having to write another check the next time I came to Pangai.

While we were serving in Tonga a commercial airline was late in arriving to Tonga on a Saturday night and had to unload passengers and also load additional fuel so that they could fly on to New Zealand. The fueling vehicle had a flat tire so they did not get the plane ready to depart before midnight. When the clock struck mid-night all the lights of the airport were turned off and the workers, including the air-traffic controllers, started leaving the airport. What you had was a planeload of people sitting on the runway who were not allowed to fly out of Tonga. They had to call a special session of some of the parliament to pass emergency legislation to allow the plane to leave Tonga. The people sat on the plane for over three hours to get a bill passed to turn on the airport lights and allow the plane to take off for New Zealand.

Tongan Folk Tales

The Tongans are great story tellers, and they have many folk tales. They use these tales to teach ideals and customs. At one time it was a nightly practice to tell these tales to the children at bedtime called *po fananga*. These tales are also often told during the social drinking of kava known as *fai kava*. Because the Tongans tell these orally the style of the tales are never the same and are ever morphing.

One day we went to the bush with Valoa, one of our eiki vaka, and Doctor Skankey and Alice to show what a typical Tongan garden looked like. While we toured the bush, Valoa told the Tongan tale of catching sharks. They prepare a pole with a noose at the end of it. Using a dead dog as both bait on the pole and chum in the water, they sing a chant to entice the special white shark named *Hina* to come. When Hina comes, they throw a wreath made of a special plant into the water to honor Hina. They then instruct Hina to go and get the other sharks. Hina swims off and then returns with other sharks following. As the sharks pass by the boat they leap through the noose, which the fishermen cinch up. The captured shark is deposited in the boat. They continue doing this until they have enough sharks. Then they thank Hina and she goes on her way. Dr. Skankey's comment about the tale was, "I knew they kept dogs around for some good reason."

Another prominent folk tale deals with whirlwinds and tornadoes. They say that Malapo, a town in Tongatapu that is alleged to have had most of these kinds of storms, is the setting for this Tongan folk tale. According to the tale, there was a rock buried in the town cemetery that turned into a blind young man who would run like a whirlwind through the islands, hitting things because he could not see them. A few years later, a warrior in the village decided to go in search of the boy. On his way to the graveyard, a large male pig told him that if he took his bush knife to a certain place in the village and pulled on a couple of bushes, the earth would open up and he would find a woman living there that would teach him how to avoid whirlwinds or tornados. He went to the designated place and pulled on the bushes, and sure enough the earth opened up to reveal a beautiful young woman. He grabbed her by the hair and was about to behead her when she awoke and spoke to him. She told him that if he would let her live, she would tell him how to avoid whirlwinds or tornados. He consented, and she then revealed that if a person would beat on a drum or piece of metal whenever a storm of this nature approached, the blind young man who created these whirlwinds and tornados would veer off and avoid them. So that is what the old Tongans believe you can do as the whirlwind or tornado approaches to get it to change its path. Some of the old-timers in these islands told stories of applying this approach and actually causing a storm to change directions.

The culture becomes one of the meaningful growth experiences of a senior missionary. Understanding the culture helps to draw you closer to the people because you better understand their behavior and the meanings in their language. When you are interested and learn about their culture they feel that you care about them. A closeness comes from "feeling aware of how another culture feels from the standpoint of an insider. This we have rather loosely called 'having empathy.' The spiritual assurance that the people are God's children, that they are of infinite worth to Him, and that his work and glory is to exalt them in his presence is the beginning of true empathy." (Eric B. Shumway, Building Cultural Differences, *Ensign*, July 1997)

The King and I and Sandy

Wherefore, I the Lord . . . gave commandments . . . That the fullness of my gospel might be proclaimed by the weak and the simple unto the ends of the world, and before kings and rulers.

Doctrine & Covenants 1:17–18, 23

When we arrived in Ha'afeva in February 1998, construction was underway on a wharf on the far side of the island. Funded by the governments of Australia and New Zealand, the wharf would enable the large inter-island ships to dock and unload much larger cargo than the fishing boats had been able to transport back to shore, such as vehicles. When we arrived there were no motorized vehicles of any kind on the island—only a horse-drawn cart. While it was a blessing, it also limited agricultural activity on the island. Also, the inter-islands boats always arrived in Ha'afeva in the middle of the night, and the noise kept everyone in the village awake whether or not they had passengers or cargo arriving. With the wharf on the far side of the island from the village, the noise from the traffic would be limited, allowing those not receiving passengers or cargo to sleep.

Planning for a King

As the completion of the wharf drew near, the village and the entire Lulunga District began to make preparations for a big celebration to dedicate the wharf. King Taufa'ahau Tupou IV was coming to be part of the dedication, which created quite a stir—he had never before visited the village of Ha'afeva. The village began to hold a regular town meeting called a *fono* to plan the dedication. Because of my role as district president, I was invited to participate. It was an interesting morning of sitting the floor for hours with our legs crossed. The meetings were so long even the Tongans were stiff when they stood up.

The fono here in Ha'afeva was different from fonos in other villages, because the Lulunga District Governor, Havealeta, lived in the town, and he directed the meeting instead of the town officer. Each of the meetings opened and closed with a prayer from one of the ministers. Everyone except our Church members sing the same songs, so when they sing a song as part of the prayer, it didn't matter who the minister was as long as they weren't LDS. Most of the discussion and questions were carried on by the ministers of Churches that were in the same capacity as I was, the District President. They seemed to be the voice for the people of their Church. The main difference was that they were also the ministers of the local congregations.

Many of the discussions dealt with how many *pola*, or food on woven palm leaves, were to be prepared for the feast. Then there was a lengthy discussion about the pig that was to be given to the king. Making a gift of a pig is a very important Tongan tradition that has been handed down over many generations. It's as big a gesture as an American giving someone a car. In this case, the Governor of Ha'apai, the larger jurisdiction over Lulunga government district, had returned a pig that had been given to him by Ha'afeva because he felt sorry for the poverty of the people. He'd said that they could use the pig he'd returned as a gift for the king. In one of the meetings it was resolved that a man who had been out of town would give his very large pig, *puaka toho*, to the king and that the other pig would be returned to the Governor of Ha'apai with thanks, which would keep the pride of the village of Ha'afeva intact.

The meetings also dealt with the type of entertainment that would be provided from each of the villages in the Lulunga government district. Entertainment in Tonga is generally the cultural dances.

Dancing is still very much a traditional affair and an important part of the culture of the kingdom of Tonga. It is an art in which complex arm and body movements are visual extensions and enhancements of the sung poetry. The movements help viewers achieve a more profound understanding of the text.

During these meetings a request was made for the king to stay in our Church building since it was the only place on the island, other than our house, that had running water and indoor plumbing. I consented to its' use but told them that I would have to clear this with the mission president and also the PBO. The Church leaders were very excited when I talked to them about the king staying in the Church building. He would be staying in a large room on the ocean side of the Church building that was often used for district council meetings. The PBO informed me that they would need to do some maintenance on the building so that it would be in good condition and give a good image of the Church. To that end, they would send up people to do the maintenance as soon as possible. The Area Presidency said that if a special bed was needed for the king they would have one sent from New Zealand, but the king ended up bringing his own.

A plan was made for the village of Ha'afeva to present a *lakalaka*, the national dance of Tonga. This required intense preparation. There were practices two to three times a week for almost two months. I decided to participate in the *lakalaka* because I had performed in a *lakalaka* for Queen Salote, the mother of the current king, during my first mission in 1958. At that time our branch in Pangai, Ha'apai, had just returned from the annual mission conference in Nuku'alofa, were we had presented a *lakalaka* about Joseph Smith. When Queen Salote came to her summer home in Pangai, the branch members decided that we should present our *lakalaka* to her, especially because I, a palangi, was dancing. Queen Salote presented me with a special large double woven mat for my participation, which I still have over fifty years later.

Preparing the Church Property

To coordinate the preparations of the Church property, I was trying to keep in contact with the PBO about what and who they would be sending to fix up the chapel. This was easier said than done. There was only one phone in the village, and it was operated by the Tongan government out of a small, run-down office with a single clerk who placed and received all phone calls. People had to wait in line to tell the clerk who they wished to speak to. If he couldn't get the person right away, you had to go to the end of the line of people and wait again. This was very frustrating because the people I wanted to talk to at the PBO often either weren't there or were busy, and I would have to go to the end of the line to try again. One day I went through an entire list of people at the PBO and got no one. In frustration, I told the clerk to ask for Gordon B. Hinckley. When he said, "Is Hinckley there?" Sandy, who was sitting outside with all the women, just about fell off the steps. But I got the man I wanted to talk to immediately. Maybe they thought I was serious.

That same night they sent five men on one of the inter-island boats to start the work, including two cleaners, an electrician, a plumber, and a carpenter. They arrived the next day with all kinds of equipment. The next few days the Churchyard was humming with activity and noise. They power washed the chapel with water inside and out and did general maintenance work to make the building suitable for the king.

The villagers were extremely busy weaving mats and making other preparations for the royal visit. A tall arch for the king to enter through had to be built over the gate to the Church property. They built two other arches for the dedication—one by the wharf and one leaving the bush and coming into the village. It was said that the king could not walk the distance from the front gate to the chapel, so the PBO workers also had to modify the Church gate so that the king's suburban could drive right up to the doors. This required us to move of one of the chain-link fence's posts and remove all the plants along the sidewalk leading up to the chapel doors After the metal fence post was moved, we realized we'd forgotten about the large side-view mirrors on the suburban. The workers wanted to take out the entire front gate again to make room. I suggested removing one of the side-view mirrors on the Suburban to avoid the extra work, but they claimed that no one had the right to alter the king's car without his permission. After some lengthy discussions, I let them cut the fence on one side and alter it sufficiently for the side-view mirrors to clear it, on the condition that they put it back like it was after the celebration. It would have taken ten minutes to remove the side-view mirrors, but instead they spent hours changing the gate.

Mixed Messages and Confusion

Many people in the village tried to take charge of planning the celebration, which became very confusing and frustrating to say the least. The son of the noble for the island tried to take charge. It really was a town event, but he was *fielahi*, a person who wanted to be big and important. Some of the people called him a *fiekai mu'a*, or someone who wanted to eat at the table with all of the renowned guests. Changes were being constantly being made, and it was hard to know "who was on first" sometimes. Veiongo, the wife of the noble, asked us to have the Australian ambassador stay in our house. The mayor said that maybe the New Zealand ambassador would also stay here, if they didn't mind staying together. The son of Veiongo, on the other hand, said that the ambassadors would stay somewhere else and the daughter of the premier and her husband would stay at our house. We thought it should be the ambassadors. Since their countries financed the wharf, it didn't seem right to put them in a house where there wasn't any plumbing just to put the daughter of someone who hadn't really had anything to do with the project in our house. As it turned out, none of the dignitaries stayed at our house.

With the king staying at our Church building, the original plan was to have the feast and entertainment also at the Church premises, but that plan was suddenly changed. The mayor and his committee decided they wanted to have the feast at the other end of town. While no reason for the change was given, we believed that it was because they wouldn't be able to smoke on Church property. It actually turned out for the best, as the Church property would have been crowded with tents and people.

The whole dedication celebration was growing bigger by the minute. Suddenly, we were notified that the Queen might also be coming, which did not happen. It was also announced that there would be live television coverage to Tongatapu and they would make a video of it. Sandy wrote the children and told them "Just think, Dad will be on live television dancing in a skirt." You wouldn't believe how many people there were in town, and in addition there were two trucks, a tractor with a trailer running up and down the streets, and the loader, the roller, and the grader. We knew we would be glad when all the traffic left and the village became quiet again. We thought what an adjustment it would be to come back to America with all the traffic in Washington!

The night before the king was to arrive, a loader and grader—which had been shipped in by way of the new wharf—ran all night grading the road to the new location. Our Branch President turned on the noisy generator at 2:30 a.m. for the Church property lights because the ladies of the village had told him they wanted to come over at that time and start decorating the room where the king was to stay. The women didn't show up as they decided it was best to wait for Veiongo. She was due in at the same time as the king.

The Royal Police Brass Band

As part of the dedication, the king's forty-person Royal Police Brass Band came to the island. They asked to use the Church's folding chairs for their rehearsal at the elementary school. No one else had any chairs—only benches. The day before the king's arrival was my birthday, so we invited them to come to the Church outdoor cultural hall and sports court and play a concert for the village. The concert was wonderful. It started with American old-time big band tunes from 1940s. Sandy and I danced to the rock and roll and swing. It was so nostalgic I had tears in my eyes. It was like the concert was just for me on my birthday. By the end, the Tongans were having a great time dancing and being silly. We had some of the branch members over afterwards for a *lakalaka* practice and some chocolate cake.

We noted that night because Tonga is on the other side of the International Date Line, my father and I were actually celebrating our birthdays at the same time. Because the time in Tonga is one day ahead of the U.S.A. it was the 6th of August in America and the 7th of August in Tonga.

The King's Arrival

The day the king's boat arrived, Sandy cleaned house and baked four loaves of *ma hopa* and two loaves of regular bread for his arrival. Two of the ma hopa loaves were for the king. The ma hopa had a very unique taste and was a great hit with the Tongans. (Note that *ma-* is the Tonga word for bread and hopa- the name of the banana.)

Sandy had just finished it and put together a big pot of soup when, at 1:30 pm, we were told that the king had decided to stay in the Church that night instead of on his boat as had been previously scheduled, and that he would be there in an hour and a half. We nearly panicked. Veiongo still hadn't come, and she was the one who was really in charge of the king's accommodations. The women of the village still hadn't decorated the room in the Church where he was staying, and the arch over the front gate wasn't quite ready. One full-time Elder was writing "Long Live the King" on a piece of white fabric, but even that wasn't ready. The village was in the process of blowing up balloons. As soon as everyone heard the news, the preparation activities went into overdrive.

Shortly before five p.m. the king's housecleaner and another attendant came to the Church to inspect the king's accommodations. These two women said they didn't like the way the Church bathroom smelled and decided that the king should stay in our house. About this time, Veiongo finally turned up. They had a somewhat heated discussion about what to do and finally decided to move everything out of our bedroom, including our bed, and put the king in there. They emptied the room in about twenty minutes. Everything, including the clothes from the closet, went in the other bedroom. We, of course, would have to find another place to sleep. They also informed us that we should empty our refrigerator out so the king's cook could use it. While we started throwing toiletries in a bag, emptying the refrigerator, and trying to scrub the bathroom a little better, they set up the king's king-sized bed up in our bedroom.

After about thirty minutes, the leader of the military band, who also happened to be Noble Ve'ehala, came to referee the situation. He told the attendants that they were wrong to change the plans and that the king was to stay in the chapel as originally planned. The decision was based upon the fact that the noble of this island was to make the arrangements and not anyone else—even though the arrangements may not meet the requirements of the palace staff. The women of the village and young men who had helped move all of the king's things into our bedroom then left with all the king's things to go set up the room for the king back at the Church.

Picture everything removed from a bedroom—clothes, bed, dresser, tables—and stacked in the next room and the two of us standing forlorn in the middle of the house with the refrigerator empty and two nights of clothing in a bag. Everyone had left us to fend for ourselves without any expression of regrets for the inconvenience. Sandy and I were a little grumpy about the whole thing. It took us a while to see the humor in it.

We just finished putting the house back together when the king arrived and while he was making his entrance, so did the mission president, President Kivalu, and his wife, Manu. We had been wondering where they were and where they would stay. While I greeted them, Sandy was sitting on the sidewalk leading to the front door of the chapel with the other women of the village. A tapa cloth was extended the length of the sidewalk for the king to walk on. It served the similar purpose to the American red carpet that is sometimes laid out on formal occasions. Sandy was actually sitting right where the king got out of the car. Both sides of the sidewalk were lined with women sitting cross-legged on the grass.

It ended up that the President and Sister Kivalu, his counselor, the seminary director and his son all stayed in our small, three-room house. That evening, Sandy and I, along with our guests, two missionaries, the Branch President, his wife and Akesa, a neighbor member who attended the Church of Tonga, went into the Church and shared a short Monday night family home evening with the king. Only President Kivalu, his counselor, and the seminary director were allowed in the king's presence. The rest of us sat in the hall. We all sang a song, which was followed by an inspirational thought by the Seminary Director, a prayer by the President Kivalu, and another hymn. Before we left, Sister Kivalu, Sandy and I were allowed to join them. One at a time, we crawled into the room on our hands and knees and kissed or shook the king's hand. To show Tongan respect we had to crawl to be lower than the king. When we had an audience with him previously at the royal palace he was sitting in a chair on a platform and we could stand and not be higher than him.

Let the Activities Begin

It was amazing how many people came to Ha'afeva. There were kava (a drink made of a root mixed with water) parties in two of the weaving halls and a big dance going on in another. The place was jumping. It was actually very reminiscent of being on the boardwalk at the beach in America.

We went to bed very late and were sleeping soundly when there was a knock on the door about 1:30 a.m. It was a royal guard, one of the many who had been stationed around the Church for security. He said that there was a young lady at the fence that wanted to see me. It turned out to be the daughter of the branch president of Kotu. She had a bucket of mangoes as a gift. Time of night is not relevant to Polynesia.

We were awakened again at 5:45 a.m. by Valoa, one of our boat drivers, who asked me to come out in the road and participate in the *fakatakatofa*, or performing the lakalaka with the rest of the village while the king slept. It didn't disturb anyone but me because everyone else in the village was already up.

While we were eating some breakfast, one of the king's attendants requested that Sandy make two more loaves of *ma hopa* as the king liked it so much that he wanted to take some home to the queen. A food fit for a King and Queen, huh! They would now call Sandy the "Ma Hopa Queen of Tonga." Throughout the visit the king's helpers kept coming over to ask for things like our tea kettle to heat water for the king's hot chocolate, the iron and ironing board, and eggs. We complied with all their requests except for lending a toaster, which we didn't own.

The wharf dedication was nice, and we had front seats of honor. Like all of these kinds of ceremonies, it was lengthy. The king made the concluding remarks. Like most commemorative programs in

Tonga the entertainment and the food were more important than the ceremony. When the dedication was completed, we followed the band back along the road through the bush to the feast area. We waited for it to start in an area for the invited guests. When we did eat, our food was really quite American. We had delicious yams, potato salad, fried chicken, cole slaw, and watermelon—not a sign of a fish or lobster. It was quite a surprise and a little disappointing; we loved the fresh seafood of the islands.

When the eating was almost complete, the entertainment began. Our lakalaka from Ha'afeva was one of the first events. It was followed by a number of *ta'olunga* and *ma'ulu'ulu*. The village had determined that I would be placed in the honored *vahenga* position in the front row, but at the last minute they escorted the National Minister of Police, a member of the king's cabinet, to that position and placed me in the *ta'ofi vahenga*, the next-most-honored position. They placed another man on my left who was visiting from Pangai and he and the Minister of Police had no idea what to do. Sandy said all they did was stand and look at me perform. It made it hard for me because while I knew the dance, I needed an occasional clue from the really good dancers who always stood next to me at our practices. Even though you are not partners with the person next to you it does make you feel like you are dancing with a broom if they don't know the dance.

During these dances, it's customary for the audience to *pale'i* or give presents to the dancers. People were constantly coming up and sticking money or other items in my shirt or wrapping lengths tapa cloth around me or the other dancers. It's hard to dance with a cloth mat draped over you! I retained a few of the things that were given to me, including a hand-woven mat from the king, but most of the gifts were whisked away because of the large pile of things in front of me, and they never surfaced again.

After the early evening entertainment, the king swam in the ocean near the wharf as a part of opening the wharf. All the men were invited to attend as part of the celebration, but they were not allowed to swim in the same area as the king. That night there was also an open bar party to which everyone was invited.

The next morning, as the king was preparing to leave the Church, Sandy and I went to get a picture of him getting into his suburban. The king's aides motioned for us to come a little closer, so we did. There was no one else around—the villagers were all kept outside the fenced area by the royal guards. As the king exited the building, the guards motioned for us to come forward so that he could greet us. He walked with the support of two canes, so it was difficult for him to stop, stand, and shake our hands, but he did so, and in excellent English said, "Thanks so much for your help." Then he turned and entered the suburban. We thought that it was a very nice gesture on his part, but because he shook our hands we didn't get to take his picture.

The day after the king left, Veiongo, who had previously put two turkeys for her family in our gas refrigerator, told us to go ahead and eat them. We were pretty short on gas for our stove and didn't want to cook something for over three hours, so we asked the branch president and his wife to cook the turkeys in their umu and share in the meal. Veiongo had also given us some fresh vegetables for a green salad. It was like dying and going to heaven. We hadn't had a salad with tomatoes, cucumbers, green onions, carrots, green peppers, and lettuce (not cabbage) since we came into the mission field almost eight months before. It was wonderful. Sandy also made jell-o with fruit and added it to the meal. It was the first time these Tongans had ever eaten a salad or jell-o or turkey. After the meal, at about four in the afternoon, we walked back to the wharf to see the first inter-island boat dock. It was a fitting end to a very busy and sometimes frustrating week.

The whole celebration was recorded and then televised on the main island of Tongatapu. Because the king was staying in our Church building, it was prominently shown on National TV and served as good publicity for the Church throughout Tonga. The filming also presented me dancing the lakalaka, and when I returned to the island of Tongatapu people recognized me when they met me on the street in Nuku'alofa as the palangi that danced at the dedication of the wharf in Ha'afeva.

We two weak and simple ministers of the gospel were blessed to have numerous opportunities in our mission to declare the gospel in various ways to a king and ruler. We had visited with the king for a family home evening. We had also proclaimed the gospel by our actions in assisting his visit to Ha'afeva. It was truly a fulfillment, for us, of D&C 1:23: "The fulness of my gospel [will] be proclaimed by the weak and the simple unto the ends of the world, and before kings and rulers."

A Temple Trip Watched Over by Angels

❖

I have given the heavenly hosts and mine angels charge concerning you . . . And whoso receiveth you, there I will be also, for I will go before your face. I will be on your right hand and on your left, and my Spirit shall be in your hearts, and mine angels round about you, to bear you up.

Doctrine & Covenants 84:42, 88

The Lulunga District had been preparing for almost two months to make a trip to the Nuku'alofa Temple on the main island of Tongatapu. This temple trip would be different than most in the Church because it would require an eight-hour boat trip on top of the deck of an inter-island boat. Thankfully, with the completion of the new wharf, the members would be able to board the boat without having to transfer from a tiny boat in the middle of the night. The wharf was dedicated during the second week in August, and the temple trip was to take place two weeks later. The district's branch presidents were working with the members to prepare for the trip, and projected that almost ninety people, including children, would go—nearly a sixth of the members in the district. However, a lot of the members' energy had been focused on the wharf dedication in early August. They had been busy decorating the town, planning the large feast, and preparing dances for the king and other visiting dignitaries. This had a significant impact on their temple trip preparation because most of their spare time had been devoted to the dedication preparation.

With the wharf dedication over, the members settled down for serious preparation for the temple trip. Because of the remote location of the district I received special permission, as the district president, to perform the final temple interviews for the members which can usually only be done by the mission president or one of his counselors. The time was drawing near, and I had not interviewed all the members who were planning to go. Sandy and I began to worry that the dedication had diverted the members' attention from spiritual matters, and that maybe we wouldn't have as many members going to the temple as we'd planned.

Temple Interview Visits

We made a prayerful decision to take the Church boat to visit three of the six islands in the district to do the final temple interviews. To visit all three in a single day, we had to time the tides just right. Siaosi Lavaka, our eiki vaka, determined that we would leave early the next morning for O'ua, though he was concerned about the heavy storm clouds on the horizon. I told him not to worry because we were on the Lord's errand. We had prayed about this decision and knew that God would send angels to watch over us and fulfill the promise in D&C 61 that the faithful would not perish by the waters.

When we awoke in the morning, the sea was not calm. It was obvious that we were in for a difficult voyage. As I looked upon the rough seas, the words of the hymn *"Master, the Tempest Is Raging"* kept playing over and over again in my mind.

> *Master, the tempest is raging!*
> *The billows are tossing high!*
> *The sky is o'ershadowed with blackness.*
> *No shelter or help is nigh.*
> *Carest thou not that we perish?*
> *How canst thou lie asleep*
> *When each moment so madly is threat'ning*
> *A grave in the angry deep?*
> *The winds and the waves shall obey thy will:*

Peace, be still.
Whether the wrath of the storm-tossed sea
Or demons or men or whatever it be,
No waters can swallow the ship where lies
The Master of ocean and earth and skies.
They all shall sweetly obey thy will:
Peace, be still; peace, be still.

Hymns, 1985, *Master, the Tempest Is Raging,* no. 105

We prayed vocally and in our hearts that our trip would be safe and peaceful.

When we arrived in O'ua, we climbed the steep, red-clay hill from the sea to the chapel and had the branch president gather the people who were going to the temple so that I could finish their interviews. The members gathered in their small, wooden chapel and sang Church hymns and visited while I conducted the interviews in the branch president's office. Four of these people were going to the temple for the first time. When the interviews were over, we held a short meeting with the members, encouraging them to give their time and attention to spiritual as well as physical preparation for the temple trip.

As we left O'ua for the three-hour trip to the island of Nomuka, the weather became worse. We knew that the deep ocean channels on the way to Nomuka would not be kind to us. One of the windows in our boat was missing its Plexiglas, and the wind and waves that came through it soaked us. The wind howled, the spray flew, and the boat creaked and moaned as it labored up the giant waves, caught the crests, and glided forward over the top. The propeller raced each time it momentarily came out of the water. While there was some nervous fear in our hearts we knew that we were in God's hands and that angels were watching over us. The only pleasant part of the trip was seeing a few playful humpback whales spouting and breaching. They didn't seem to let the weather bother them.

We arrived at Nomuka not only very wet, but cold, as cold winds had now joined the rain and rough sea. The rough seas had made the journey take longer than we'd planned, so we gathered the Saints and performed our interviews without even changing out of our wet clothes. The winds were with us as we travelled quickly to Tungua, the final island, but the wind and the waves continued to shower us with sea water and intermittent rain beat down on us in tremendous volume.

When we arrived at Tungua we were soaked to the bone. Happily, we found that the members were holding a temple trip planning meeting in the chapel. This inspired gathering allowed us to accomplish our interviews quicker than anticipated. When I completed the interviews, there was a large puddle of water under the metal folding chair from my dripping clothes. Sandy was very chilled, and we still had an hour-long trip back to Ha'afeva.

The weather had deteriorated into a gale with fierce winds and raging seas. The hour was late, the sun was sinking rapidly, and thick, dark clouds had gathered and darkness was fast becoming our enemy. We would have to chase the dark, or *tuli he po'uli*, as they say in the islands, to return home to our beds. As we sailed home, the storm worsened. We found protection by passing close to shore on the sheltered side of a couple of uninhabited islands, where the waves and wind were less boisterous.

Finally, we arrived back in Ha'afeva, having completed our assignment of conducting temple interviews for three branches. We thanked the Lord that we had arrived safely under his watchful eye, for we knew that angels had truly been watching over us.

A Special Temple Interview

Shortly before our temple interview trip, I had a very important learning experience. One of the couples from the Ha'afeva Branch had prepared themselves to go to the temple for the first time. They were planning to be sealed to each other and to one of their children before our district temple trip. As with other members in the district, I had been given special permission to conduct the second temple recommend interview with them. I had already interviewed Sione, the husband, but I could not interview his wife, Mafi, until just before they were to board the boat for Nuku'alofa. It was late at night, and if there were any problems they would not be able to be taken care of before they sailed.

We had a very good interview and as I concluded I asked whether there was anything that I had not asked directly about that might be an issue prohibiting her from attending the temple. Her answer was, "yes."

My heart skipped a beat, and I thought to myself, "Oh, no. She has a problem, and they are going to leave this evening on the boat. How am I going to resolve this issue?" I thought through various problems she might have and tried to quickly figure out how I could handle each of them. I then asked her what the problem was. Her answer: "I am late to Church."

I don't know if I was ever so happy for someone to be late for Church. With this simple answer I was taught a very powerful principle about how important it is to examine every corner of our lives to see what we must do to be more worthy to enter the temple. That is what Mafi had done in her simple, powerful, faithful way. We talked about her tardiness, and she promised to do better in the future. I didn't say so, but I should have told Mafi that she had taught me a very powerful lesson that I would never forget. This was another example of the simple yet significant faith of the Tongan people.

The Final Preparation

The day of our temple interview trip, the seas had turned ugly all over Tonga, delaying the various inter-island boats. The storm was severe enough to stop or delay most of the shipping activities in Tonga—except for one palangi missionary couple trying to get home from temple interviews. And so, after all our preparations, the temple trip had to be delayed as well. We would have to take the *Olovaha* a day late, but at least it would dock at the new wharf for easy boarding, and the seas had calmed somewhat. Unfortunately, it appeared from the change in the boat schedules that the Saints from Nomuka would not be able to find a boat to sail to Tongatapu in time.

A few days before the temple trip, I had still not received any word about the final participation of the Matuku Branch. I felt impressed to go to Matuku and see why we hadn't heard anything from the members. I had Siaosi prepare the boat on very short notice for an early-morning trip to Matuku. When we arrived, we found that the branch president had been sick in bed for the last week and that the branch's preparations had not taken place as planned. The temple recommend forms had not been completed. The branch had also changed their travel plans to leave for the temple two days later than the rest of the district to save money on the passage, which meant they would miss two days of our temple visit. We set to work getting the recommends in order, but we left feeling very discouraged that the Matuku Branch would not travel with the main temple group and would therefore miss part of the weeklong temple experience.

The morning we prepared to leave for Tongatapu, the Saints arriving in Ha'afeva from O'ua, Tungua, and Kotu gathered at the new wharf with their supplies including food needed to feed us at the temple. Everyone was sad that the Matuku Branch members would not be coming with us. As the time drew near for the *Olovaha* to arrive, a small dot appeared on the horizon in the direction of Matuku. Everyone supposed that this boat from Matuku held nonmembers travelling to Tongatapu, but as it drew near the people shouted that it was Sione Fatai's boat and that it was filled with members. What great rejoicing from the members at the wharf as they recognized who it was! As they arrived and unloaded at the wharf, they not only unloaded people but also ice coolers full of fish. The members of the Matuku Branch had met after my visit. They had noted my disappointment in their not traveling with the rest of the district to the temple. Sione Fatai, the first counselor in the district presidency and a member of the Matuku Branch, was one of the finest divers in the Lulunga area. He had recommended that the members go diving that night for fish, lobsters, octopus, and shellfish that they could sell in Tongatapu to earn enough money to travel to the temple with the rest of the Saints. Only after the men in the branch had spent the entire night diving did they have what they thought was enough seafood to raise the money for the additional boat fare. At sunrise they returned home quickly, finished their preparations for the temple trip, jumped in Sione Fatai's boat, and sailed to the wharf in time to join the rest of the Saints.

In the somewhat calmer seas, the boat ride to the temple was a little better than it might have been, but not good enough to keep most of the passengers from getting seasick. Being on the deck was a little easier for them because they could just lean forward on the rail and "cast their bread upon the water." Sandy and I ate green mangoes and crackers and held up pretty well. While the tossing of the ship was difficult, there was no rain, so we didn't get wet riding on the deck of the boat. The boat had about two hundred passengers, and many were up on the open deck with deck-to-deck people, so to speak. It was hard to even walk. Tongans that weren't throwing up were wrapped up in blankets like cocoons. One individual on her first inter-island voyage thought that there were just a lot of stacks of blankets and bags on the deck. Imagine her surprise when the boat stopped, and suddenly all the bags and blankets began to move.

The boat left Ha'afeva two hours late, and the difficult seas made it take an hour longer than usual to sail to Nuku'alofa. It was almost dark in Tongatapu when we docked. According to ship's rules we could not claim any of our baggage in the heart of the ship until everything else was unloaded, which took almost ninety minutes.

President Kivalu had arranged for two Liahona High School buses to pick us up and take us to the temple housing. They had bread, butter, jam, and a warm chocolate drink called *milo* waiting for us when we arrived at the motel. Bread, butter and jam are food not available on our small islands, and was a very thoughtful gift from President Kivalu. It was after nine p.m. before people got settled. Interestingly, if the Nomuka Saints had come with us, there would have been a problem—we had reserved twenty rooms, but the temple housing only had fourteen available when we arrived. In hindsight, the storm may have been part of the Lord's plan.

We were now ready for temple work. We knew that angels had watched over us in our preparations and travel and that, according to Elder Vaughn J. Featherstone, "all who faithfully attend to temple work [have] unseen angels watch over [their] loved ones." (Royden G. Derrick, *Temples in the Last Days*, 103)

The Temple Experience—A Preparation for Tribulation

❖

The Saints in this temple district will be better able to meet any temporal tribulation because of this temple. Faith will increase as a result of the divine power associated with the ordinances of heaven and the assurance of eternal associations.

President Ezra Taft Benson, *Teachings of Ezra Taft Benson*, Bookcraft, 1998, 254

Sometimes inspiration or revelation happens to us and we fail to recognize it. One manifestation of inspiration occurred in connection with the members from Nomuka. While it was a small thing, it does show how the Lord works with small pieces of inspiration. Just before we sailed to the temple, we sent a telegram to the branch president suggesting that they try to get to the temple on the *Lana Fo'ou*, a boat from Nomuka, which was sailing the day after we had. If they could get on that boat, they were to call the mission office and let them know. When we got to Tongatapu, no word had been received from Nomuka and we figured that they were not coming.

Our little piece of inspiration happened on Saturday, while Sandy and I were in town doing some personal things after attending the temple. Sandy wanted to go to the little flea market that was held at the wharf every Saturday. While we were there, we decided to go visit the person in charge of the *Eagle*, the boat that we hoped to sail back to Ha'afeva on. In talking to the person in charge, we learned that the Nomuka Saints were coming on the *Loto Ha'angana* in about three hours. They had managed to get one of the larger boats to pick them up from their island, something that particular boat did not normally do. The spirit of inspiration surely guided us on this side trip; we found out that the Nomuka Saints were coming and had enough time to arrange transportation to the temple for them.

We also found that we'd been inspired in choosing the date of our temple trip. Though we didn't know it before hand, we found that the temple was open all night on the last Friday of the month—the same Friday we were there. These extra hours allowed some of the families with children to trade off having one spouse attend the temple while the other one slept or cared for the children. We couldn't have picked a better time to accommodate the work that we had come to do.

We stayed in temple housing across the street from the temple. It had a simple but large Tongan-style kitchen for preparing group meals. Though each branch was prepared to provide its own meals, members from all over Tongatapu brought food to those in temple housing. They knew how many members were visiting and that many of them were very poor, so instead of simple food they brought cases of chicken. When they found out that the Matuku Saints had brought fish to sell, they also came to buy. One ward made arrangements to send a bus on Sunday to pick us up for Church, and they provided a meal for us after the meetings.

Many of the members who had completed their family pedigree charts and family group sheets during Doctor Skankey's visit in June brought family names to the temple. Little did they understand the great blessing this would be for them when they filled out those papers.

A family history missionary couple, Elder and Sister Hurd, who were in charge of the family history center, were very accommodating to us. We brought many pedigree charts with us to be made temple ready. The family history center was normally closed on Saturday so the temple work could not be made temple ready. Elder and Sister Hurd took the sheets in on Sunday and did all the data entry work that day and took it over to the temple before 6 a.m. on Monday so the people could do the work on some of the names before they had to leave Tuesday. Because the temple was only open half day on Monday, the extra effort of the missionary couple was a special blessing.

None of these people had ever done work for their own family, and it was a very special and spiritual experience for them to serve as proxies for these ancestors or officiate in their baptisms. Some of them were so overcome by emotion that they could not speak the words of the baptismal prayer. One brother who was observing the baptisms for the dead said, "The next time we come to the temple I am going to make sure that I bring some of my own family names so that I can know this great joy of doing the work for the kindred dead."

The only problem we had was a marriage verification problem with two couples who were to be sealed. Their membership records did not show a marriage date. Without this, the temple required that the couples provide proof of marriage. This proved to be a big challenge for one couple as they had been married for over twenty years. We called to the government offices in Ha'apai where they were married and they couldn't find any information because the couple couldn't remember the year of their marriage. They gave us one year and then after a search for their marriage documentation they realized that was the year their first son was born and that could not have been the correct year. We were unsuccessful in finding proof, and while they were able to attend the temple, they left without being sealed together and to the large number of children that were there with them. The other couple had been married on Tongatapu, so we were able to take them to the police station in the government district and get a copy of the official marriage document. They were then sealed in the temple as a family.

In our conversations with members during the temple trip, we discovered that most of the people in the Lulunga District had never received their patriarchal blessings. There is no patriarch assigned to the district so it had just never happened. The Seminary Supervisor that came during the king's visit to Ha'afeva was a patriarch so we made it a point to see him while we were in Tongatapu and he agreed to come and stay for a few days whenever we needed him and give patriarchal blessings. We knew what a blessing it would be (literally and figuratively) to have him come. We started to talk about patriarchal blessings in each of the branches and explain what they are and invited the people to get theirs. This is just another of the "little" things that these people have not received for all these years.

The temple trip was a wonderful success. Seventy-five members and children participated, eight people received their endowments, and four families were sealed together. Our first day in the temple was a record-setting day for the Nuku'alofa Temple. In addition to our eight members, individuals from Vava'u, Tonga, and Suva, Fiji, also received their own endowments.

The Fast Sunday after the temple trip was very revealing and uplifting. We received many reports on the testimonies that the members of the branches bore about the great experience that they had on the temple trip. Many of the people were very emotional about their experience. I am sure that the temple work they did has had a lasting impression on them, laying a foundation for a more valiant effort in the future.

This experience was one of the many fulfilling spiritual experiences that we enjoyed during our mission. It unified the Lulunga District. The missionary couple that replaced us there took the temple work to another level by making a weeklong trip to the temple each quarter. I am sure that this regular attendance at the temple has served as one of the tools of the Lord to help prepare these great people of the Lulunga District to be a Stake of Zion someday.

Prayers and Fasting
End Drought

❖

Most of you, I assume, have fasted and prayed with a
purpose—that you might find answers to perplexing
personal problems or the needs of others, or that moisture
might fall..I believe that the Lord will hear our earnest
supplications, if we will back up our fasting and prayers
with goodness in our lives.

Elder Gordon B. Hinckley, *Teachings of Gordon B.*
Hinckley, Deseret Book Co., 1997, 237

Little did we realize that the temple trip would also prepare the
members to meet the temporal tribulations of a serious drought.
We were aware that we hadn't had any rain for a while, but we didn't
think too much about it. At first, we simply noted that a lot of the
people in the village had been coming to the Church *sima*, or concrete
cistern, to fill five-gallon water containers to use in their homes. The
neighbors next door used our water for all their cooking, laundry,
and showering, but they had done this for some time. While we were
glad to help, it bothered us that this neighbor's wife had recently gone
inactive to attend the Church of Tonga. But then the branch
president's family also began using the Church sima for most of their
needs. A lot of water had been used for showering and power washing
the inside and outside of the Church building before the king came,
but we hadn't thought it a problem at the time. Now, when people

from other islands came to catch the big boat, and they showered in the outdoor Church shower we became more and more concerned. The Branch President cleaned the chapel one day and told us there was a toilet that was running continuously. We couldn't afford waste like that—we hadn't had any significant rain since May.

We realized we had a water shortage one morning when Sandy had just started shampooing her hair and the water stopped. We tried to pump water up to our little water tower, but this time it didn't work. Luckily, Sandy managed to rinse her hair and finish showering with a single gallon of water. We checked the big cement sima, and sure enough, it was so close to empty that we couldn't pump any water up to our water tank. We then checked the other two smaller, metal simas. They were also dry. This meant no water at all on Church property. We managed to get a large trash can full of water from our neighbor Siliote's sima, but we knew we would have to be very careful about how we used our water. We began learning how to live on one gallon of water a day for all our washing, showering, cooking, and toilet flushing. We had been praying for a week or so for rain. Now we began fasting, too. We even began writing home and asking our family and friends to remember the drought in their prayers. At first this was just a unique experience, albeit a great inconvenience, but that changed quickly.

Another week passed without rain. We were still using the neighbor's water. It was amazing how far a cup of water could go—Sandy bragged that she could wash the dishes from an entire meal in a cup of water. If she used soap, it took a second cup to rinse them. We used about half of a three gallon- bucket of water to bathe. Sandy would bath first so there was no shaving cream in the water. We would stand in the shower and use handfuls of water or a wash cloth to rinse. We'd expected to bathe this way before we came, but it was quite an adjustment after getting used to indoor plumbing and the solar water-heating system.

The worst part was the toilet. We poured water down the toilet to flush it, but we were obliged to let quite a bit of waste collect before we finally did so. We saved all the water we used for washing clothes or dishes or bathing to flush the toilet, but we could often only flush it once a day. The smell was not wonderful. I used the neighbor's outhouse a few times, but it was so dirty that I told Sandy she shouldn't even try it. The neighbor did clean off the toilet seat so that it was somewhat white and not dirty brown.

Needless to say, we continued praying and fasting for rain. We received news that Nuku'alofa had received so much rain recently that the streets were like rivers, but none of it came to the Lulunga District. We were doing okay with the water from Siliote's sima, but her whole extended family, as well as a few others in the village, were also using her water, and we didn't want to run her sima dry. She felt obligated to give us the water because her sima had been filled by water from the rain gutters on our house. The church constructed the gutters to run to her sima because of all the help she'd given to our missionaries in the past. We did at least put a lock on her sima's water spout so that people couldn't use it without permission.

We asked the PBO to send us supplies to build an outhouse in the far corner of the Church property. I also casually mentioned that the Church's rain gutters needed a little bit of maintenance work. They told us they'd send two plumbers on the next boat from Nuku'alofa to build us an outhouse for emergencies and conferences. We thought it was funny that they were sending plumbers to put in an outhouse, but maybe they were experts in digging holes. On the other hand, an outhouse with plumbing wouldn't be so bad!

But when they came, they only brought the supplies to redo rain gutters, which was an overkill—they just needed to be patched up. There were no supplies for putting in an outhouse. Instead, they brought a couple of shovels to dig a well. They said that in a week or two a pump would come to pump water up from the well to the tower. There were three problems with this idea. First and foremost, it would take another week or two. Second, the water from the well was dirty and not as safe to drink as water from the sima. Third, there wouldn't be enough water in the well to meet all of our needs. The previous well had been covered over for those very reasons. I was upset. I'd asked for an outhouse, and I'd gotten rain gutters and a well. I'd only mentioned the rain gutters as a side note, hoping to fix a couple of leaks so that we didn't lose water when it did rain.

Another week passed with only *uha loi*, or a few sprinkles rain—not enough to even get you wet if you were standing outside. The PBO guys dug an eighteen-foot well and encased the walls with four fifty-gallon drums that they hammered together lengthwise. The pump arrived a week later. In the meantime, Sandy gave them hot Milo every morning and boiled *ufi* in the middle of the afternoon because there was no place to buy a meal in Ha'afeva. Fortunately, they were very nice, and the first PBO men we'd seen that had consistently worked full days. It was extra meals to fix, but for the most part was not a problem. As they say in Tonga "We needed the blessing."

Because some of the pump parts took an extra week to arrive, the plumbers stayed much longer than we expected. It would have been much easier for the PBO to just send the materials for an outhouse and have had someone in Ha'afeva do the work, but they didn't. I later learned that the Church construction handbook does not allow outhouses on Church property, which was why they built the well instead.

More time passed and there was still no rain, though we had lots of cloudy days. We were doing laundry by hand because the machine used too much water, and we were really looking forward to getting back to regular flushing!

During a visit to the island of Tungua, we were told that the people on the island of Kotu had come and asked for water from the Church sima. The simas in Kotu were all dry, and the wells there were *kona*, which meant they were either too dirty to use or gave salt water. In Ha'afeva we had least had some water.

When the well was finally completed, we were able to get some well water out of the faucet for washing dishes and out of the shower-head for filling our bathing bucket. We were still very sparing with our water, but we could now flush when we needed to. For that we were most grateful!

We had some small "false" rains off and on, and our sima now had a little water in it. Though it appeared that our prayers were helping, the drought wasn't over yet. The villagers' gardens were drying up, and it appeared that there would soon be a food shortage on some of the islands, though we knew we could survive on coconut milk, fish, and food brought from Tongatapu. We were fortunate to live on Ha'afeva;

it was not as bad off as some of the other islands. Women in O'ua were washing clothes in the ocean because they were saving all their fresh water for drinking. Their island was too high to build a well. We heard on the radio that the Vava'u island group was selling water by the barrel. We began praying that the governor would be able to get water to those islands that didn't have any and come up with some creative solutions to the food problems. Finally, the government sent some soldiers on small boats with drums of water to distribute to the people, but it wasn't enough. They eventually sent an oil tanker filled with fresh water to fill the large community simas on O'ua, Tungua, and Kotu.

We had a couple of rains that lasted an hour or so, which gave our sima enough water to take care of the upcoming district conference but not enough to share with the whole village. We locked the sima, grateful that we still had well water for rinsing dishes, washing clothes, and flushing the toilet.

The Halverson Visit

Elder and Sister Ronald T. Halverson from the area presidency and President and Sister Kivalu provided a special spiritual uplift at our district conference. A hundred and one members attended the general meeting, which was very good considering that the children who usually made up a quarter of our congregations were in school. Because they were cautious about their trip on a little boat, the meeting started over an hour late, and we had to cancel the planned visit to some of the branch buildings to explain needed maintenance and improvements.

We told Elder Halverson of the drought in the district, and he felt moved by the Holy Ghost to offer a special prayer after the regular conference meetings. We counseled together and asked the Saints to stay after the close of the final session for the special prayer, which they did. Elder Halverson asked the Lord to send rain and break the drought. He didn't promise that it would rain, but he did plead that the Lord would grant our petition. He said he didn't know why the rain was being withheld, but he repeated the plea. The moment Elder Halverson completed his prayer, we all knew that it would surely be answered and that the Lulunga people would be blessed with sufficient rain. Calm rested upon us and drowned out our worry.

The Halversons were very brave souls to visit Ha'afeva, especially since it was the first time that Sister Halverson had ever been on the ocean. She was a real trooper to make the trip. She tasted all the seafood treats the members had to offer, but Elder Halverson wasn't quite so adventurous with the food. Sister Halverson was very concerned about the leftovers from the feast the members prepared for them after the conference. She knew they didn't have much food because of the drought, and after we had finished eating, the food looked like it had hardly been touched. Sandy had just finished reassuring her that nothing ever went to waste in the village when a man came around the corner with a cooler full of food in a wheelbarrow. He wasn't a member of the Church, but his family had helped prepare some of the food, and he took some leftovers home to share with them. Sister Halverson was so taken aback by him that she asked to take his picture to help her remember her special experience in Ha'afeva.

In an article in the *New Era,* Elder Halverson recounted his feeling about this special spiritual experience. "I thought to myself, 'What faith!' They had been fasting and they asked if we would join them in a prayer for rain, which we did.

"After the conference had ended and we prepared to leave, the people on the island prayed not only for rain, but they prayed that we would have good weather until we arrived back to our destination. We got into our boats and traveled back with good weather. But as we arrived at our final destination the heavens opened and the islands were blessed with rain.

"That's the kind of faith many Polynesian people have and the kind of miracles they bring about. They have a simple faith, a deep faith." (Elder Ronald T. Halverson, "The Heavens Rained," *New Era,* Aug. 2004, 44)

Right after the conference visitors had departed, I was walking down the road when I met one of the non-members in the village. He said, "Well, I guess the drought will soon be over since one of your Church leaders has come here and prayed for rain." He wasn't a member of our Church, but he understood the significance of the prayer Elder Halverson offered.

This and all of our prayers and fasting were answered with three days of heavy, constant rain. It's amazing how little things become so wonderful. Hearing water run into the sima was a thing of joy. Our sima system was now about two-thirds full, and we were watching it closely. I calculated that it takes seven inches of rain to completely fill our system.

The storm came from the north and seemed to pause and then reverse direction to make sure the prayers of every affected islander were fully and adequately answered. The simas were now completely full and overflowing. Sandy claimed that since the rain came from the North it must have been sent through the prayers of our ward members in Oakton, Virginia.

The Elders were like two little boys playing in the water overflowing out of the sima. They shampooed their hair and washed their shirts and ran back and forth in the rain. The next morning, the village kids, Sandy, and I were doing the same things! The Tongans call this playing in the rain *faka'uha*. It was *great*! Sandy shampooed her hair at the sima with the rainwater, humming "I Think the World is Glorious and Wondrous as Can Be." It was wonderful to use clean, fresh-smelling water. The well water we had been using had that "lake" smell. Sandy thought that the smell was more of a sewer smell.

What a difference the two weekends of rain made in the islands. The grass was green again and growing really fast. We hadn't really realized how brown everything had gotten. We had people coming over to the Church property to wash their hair and shower—fully clothed, of course—in the water running out of the *sima* overflow pipe. One family even did a little laundry. We offered our thanks to all our family and friends for their prayers and fasting and to Elder Halverson for his special blessing.

The drinking situation was relieved substantially, but the late rains meant that the village wouldn't be able to harvest its usual crop in December. The government and the Church would have to provide some food relief. I began preparing lists of member families and gathering letters from each branch president detailing the specific needs of their branches. The lists generally contained the basics of flour, sugar, and rice, along with some corned beef or canned fish. In October, the main source of food for the children was mangoes, and in November, it would be breadfruit. Luckily, there was still plenty of fish, shellfish, and other seafood.

I believe that because of the temple trip, the faith of the Saints of the Lulunga District was increased and they were able to meet the temporal tribulation of this drought with greater faith without significant impact on their lives. They knew that while times might be difficult the Lord would be with them. Their earnest supplications were heard because they backed up their fasting and prayers with goodness. One of the blessings of fasting noted by Isaiah is that "the Lord shall guide thee continually, and satisfy thy soul in drought . . . and thou shalt be like a watered garden, and like a spring of water, whose waters fail not" (Isaiah. 58:11). Our souls were satisfied because we knew that the Lord had heard our prayers and accepted our fasts.

A Medical Mission?

[Missionaries] are there to heal the suffering people, to teach the gospel of Christ, to give encouragement and strength and hope and faith. They are there to heal wounds of misunderstanding and contention. They are there to bless the sick and to help those with diseased bodies and frustrated minds . . . They are living humbly among the poor, down at the level of the people but standing straight and tall to lift with strong hands.

President Gordon B. Hinckley, "The Healing Power of Christ," *Ensign*, November 1988, 52

As a mother of six children, Sandy had experienced many medical emergencies in our family. I can't count the number of times that we took a child to the emergency room. She knew that when you have active children you will experience sundry accidents that not only require a physician's attention but also a good first aid kit. We knew that medical assistance might not be close to where we served in Tonga, so we arrived on our mission with a nice first aid kit and a lot of over-the-counter medications like Ibuprofen. We knew that we were there to bless the sick spiritually as well as physically, but we didn't view ourselves as medical missionaries.

Soon after we arrived in Ha'afeva, we had experiences with two sick people looking for medicine to cure what they called a relapse, which meant starting to feel bad again soon after being sick. They had an old bottle that was hand-labeled *vai kita*, or "recovery water." We thought that it was some kind of special medicine that came from the local doctor, but we found out that it was just a local concoction that was sold over the counter. They were looking for something of the same nature that came from America. We probably should have told them that the snake medicine man and his wagon had already left town. Instead, we gave them some Ibuprofen and told them to rest. Sandy joked that we should send them a bill requesting payment in coconuts, fish, or better yet, lobster.

It wasn't long before Sandy became known as the cut doctor of Ha'afeva. Her fame spread to other islands in the district. Nuku Folau came from O'ua to have a three-inch-long cut over her eye stitched up. It would have probably required at least ten stitches in America. The local physician's assistant was, as usual, out of town, so she came to Sandy after a little encouragement from people who knew of the other fixing up Sandy had done. Sandy had to make three large butterfly bandages to close the wound. The woman told "nurse Banks" that her family had poured kerosene on the wound to stop the bleeding, which was the first time we had ever heard of such treatment. The thought of it makes me cringe even now. When she later went to see the doctor, he asked her who had put the bandage on her. She told him Sister Banks, and he wouldn't even look at the wound. He said she should just go back to see her to get a new bandage put on. We never found out whether he was upset at what Sandy had done or if he had a lot of confidence in her work, but either way, it was strange.

Sandy soon moved up from cuts to breaks. Lepeka, who was then six months pregnant, came over to see us one Sunday night. Instead of coming through the gate like normal, she came the quick way—over the top of the side fence. As she jumped down, she landed on her foot wrong and thought she had broken it. Nurse Banks to the rescue! She wrapped up a cube of frozen butter in a wet dishcloth (there was no ice) and put that on the ankle to reduce the swelling. She then applied an elastic wrap around the ankle and foot. After Lepeka watched a video with her foot propped up, we helped her home. Lepeka had a neighbor who specialized in broken bones come and massage her leg.

That woman said that Sandy had saved the day. If she hadn't taken quick action, the foot would have swollen up and made it impossible to massage. After that, someone suggested that people should come and get Sister Banks if the doctor was out.

On one occasion, a mother brought her little boy, who had fallen and scraped up his face pretty badly. She had gone to the island's clinic first, but the doctor was in Tungua, so she'd been referred to us. Her son had several abrasions on his cheek and a bad cut over his eyebrow. Sandy gave him a lollipop and had his mother clean the wound with an alcohol cleaner that burned but worked great. Of course, the mother yelled at and manhandled the boy, but she finally got him pretty clean. Sandy figured it was best if the mother had the wrestling match with the young man. He was a very shy little four-year-old, and we knew he would only be more frightened if we held him down. Once the cut was clean, Sandy put three homemade butterflies on it and bandaged him up.

As we finished, the family home evening program that came on the national radio every Monday evening started, and the mother stayed and listened. She was already a member, but had started going to the Church of Tonga when she got married. She came back the next morning when Sandy changed the bandage and she promised to come back the next morning again. Sandy encouraged her to return to Church but she never did.

Thank goodness for Neosporin, Band-Aids, and experience with cuts at home. A lot of the cuts Sandy assisted with would have required stitches in the States, but in Tonga scars are a mark of valor. One man had a bad cut on his hand. After the doctor had only given him a Band-Aid, he came to us. Sandy put a butterfly bandage on the wound. He was amazed at how well and fast it healed and proceeded to praise Sandy's capabilities throughout the entire village.

Even Nurse Sandy could get sick, though. After a Nomuka trip, Sandy woke up with a rash on her leg. We had no idea where it came from, but it went almost all the way around her leg. Her foot and ankle were swollen and red, and she was sore all the way up to her groin. Several red and sore spots developed on her increasingly tender leg. We were worried that it was a rapidly spreading infection and felt strongly that she needed penicillin. I gave her a priesthood blessing on Monday night, and we began to pray that the doctor would return quickly. He finally came back on Wednesday afternoon, and we were able to get some penicillin. We told him his returning was an answer to prayer. The day after Sandy began taking the antibiotic, her leg improved dramatically. We knew that the blessing had kept her from getting seriously ill.

One of the old wives' tales of the island is that when you have the kind of rash Sandy had, and it goes all the way around the leg, the person dies. This was a very frightening tale to hear when you are having that kind of medical problem. The doctor had no idea what the rash was, and he agreed Sandy should have some penicillin, but he had no advice. We were thankful for the penicillin to assist the power of the priesthood.

We are grateful we came to Tonga prepared with life experiences and a good first aid kit. Because of these things, we were able to bless the lives of the people we had been called to serve. We realized that this is what Elder Hales had taught when he said, "Your life is your preparation. You have valuable experience. You have raised a family and served in the Church. Just go and be yourselves." (Elder Robert D. Hales, "Couple Missionaries: A Time to Serve," Ensign, May 2001, 25)

Tongan Funerals: A Return to Old Testament Times

I thought I could just as easily have been back in King David's time or in Abraham's. I felt that you can't really understand the Tongan people until you understand the Old Testament. The reverse is also true: you really don't understand the Old Testament until you've lived among and understood the Polynesian people. They truly are of the house of Israel.

Elder John H. Groberg, *In the Eye of the Storm*,
Bookcraft, Inc., 1993, 67

During the period of our mission in the Lulunga District, we had the opportunity to participate in a number of funerals. Despite the significant Christian influence that Tonga has felt over the last hundred and fifty years, funerals are still very traditional affairs of enormous cultural significance. Tongans follow a highly ritualized grieving process wholly different from western tradition with the exception of black as the prescribed color for everybody in mourning.

These funerals gave us a better understanding of what the Old Testament refers to as "weeping and wailing," or the atmosphere of sackcloth and ashes. Two traditional Tongan funerals of note were those of a long-time member on the island of Tungua and a non-member father on the island of O'ua.

Tungua Member Funeral

On a Sunday visit to Tungua, I went with the branch president and his new counselor to visit a ninety-three-year-old member, Tevita Fetu'u, who had failing health for a couple of months after a very vibrant life. He had been hoeing his garden as usual until June of that year, but his failing eyesight made him trip over things. His family convinced him to stay home and rest. As soon as he did, his health went downhill. He had been bedridden for two months and had lost his sight, but his voice was strong when we spoke, and we could tell that he was ready to return to his Father in Heaven. After our conversation, I asked if we could offer a word of prayer. I offered the prayer and I felt impressed to ask the Lord to take his spirit, but did not because I thought it might sound strange to his nonmember family members. I did, however, bless him that he would have peace and contentment.

Late the next afternoon, the Branch President knocked at our door in Ha'afeva. He was soaking wet from a very swift boat ride. He told me that Tevita Fetu'u had passed away less than twenty-four hours after we visited with him and had found real peace and contentment. Early Tuesday morning, we returned to Tungua for the funeral services, where I was to speak. I tried to get them to hold the services in the chapel, but that had never happened in the Lulunga District before, so we stood outside in the hot sun.

The graveyard in Tungua sits up on a hill overlooking the Church property. The speakers stood on the hill and the members of the Church sat on the ground nearby to sing all of the hymns and the rest of the people from the village sat off in the distance under the cover of palm trees away from the sun.

Most of the people in attendance were dressed in black clothing, and the women had combed their wild hair out. As was traditional, they wrapped themselves in tattered, dirty mats. When appearing in public during the mourning period a traditional mourning *ta'ovala* (mat wrapped around the waist) should be worn. And when attending the funeral itself, it is obligatory. What kind of mat is worn depends on the relationship to the deceased. Close relatives who are "inferior", in kinship terms, or "brother's" side, wear old, large, frayed, coarse, torn mats, and of a large weave, sometimes even old floor mats that suit their lowly position. The bigger and dirtier the mats the more respectful they appear. These are the relatives who do the hard, menial or dirty work of preparing the umu at the funeral are known as *liongi*. Relatives on the "sister's side" wear fine mats, often family heirloom mats. Those who are not related at all should wear fine mats that are *faka'ahu*, or smoked over a fire until they are a rich mahogany color.

A number of the attendees had obviously thrown dust on their hair. Most of the weeping and wailing had taken place before we arrived for the funeral service, but there was still a continual, hysterical howling of "Oi, Oi, Oiauee" as Tevita was laid to rest.

My sermon focused on the plan of salvation. I used a glove to explain the doctrine of the body and the spirit and what happens at birth and death by putting the glove on and off. This visual aide, I felt, would help overcome some of my language weaknesses. The sermon was well received, though one minister from another Church got up and left when I started. We assumed he didn't want to hear "Mormon" doctrine.

O'ua Non-Member Funeral

We went to bed early one evening and were enjoying our sleep when, about 3:30 a.m., we heard "Banke, Banke!" coming through our bedroom louver window. A young man was calling to us. He said that his grandfather had passed away and that we were to come to the island of O'ua at 5:00 p.m. that day for the funeral. He then said that his father had sent him to ask us for 40 liters of benzene but he was not able to explain why, except that it had something to do with the funeral. We dreaded hearing the word benzene because we experienced so many challenges connected with the use and borrowing of benzene.

I put on my robe, grabbed the flashlight, went to the benzene room, and pumped forty liters of benzene for him. By this time I was so wide awake that I had a hard time going back to sleep. I tossed and turned until about 5:30 a.m. and then slept until almost 8:00 a.m. When we told our boat driver, Valoa, about the funeral, we learned that we needed to leave at 1:00 p.m. to catch the high tide and avoid the reef around O'ua. Our Church boat had a hole being repaired, so this trip had to be made in a rented smaller boat that was less protected from the sea spray.

In chatting with people before we left for O'ua, I realized that we needed to bring a gift of food to the funeral. Food is the best thing to bring to a funeral in Tonga because many family and friends of the deceased will come and stay for days, weeks, or even months. There is an old Tongan saying that explains that while the people weep and wail sincerely for the loss the deceased, they weep and wail even more because they know that they will have to feed everyone in the village for a while. I dashed to the local "seven-eleven", which was a store that had between seven and eleven shelves of merchandise, and purchased a three-pound can of corned beef. Valoa purchased a fifty-pound sack of flour. It pricked my conscience that the poor man gave his all while I, the rich man, gave only a small can of corned beef. Valoa's daughter-in-law and another woman also joined us. They brought the traditional gifts of a mat, some fabric, a tapa cloth, and some artificial flowers.

Off we sailed with the two women down under cover and Sandy and I sitting out in the open. It is what we preferred as the fresh air was wonderful and we really didn't mind getting wet. Sandy had started wearing one of her polyester dresses to travel in as it dried almost as soon as we were out of the boat.

It was the beginning of whale season, so we kept our eyes open, hoping to get a picture of one leaping out of the water. When we were almost to O'ua, Valoa reported a dead whale out in the water. This was very unusual. I tried to see it, but could only see what appeared to be a big rock. Valoa took a little side trip, and it was indeed a dead whale lying on its side against the reef. It was huge—about 35 or 40 feet long—and judging by the smell and the way the underside had been eaten away by sharks, it had been there for some time. We learned later that the O'ua Branch President had walked out on the reef and pulled out ten of the whale's teeth as souvenirs. A piece of one of these whale bones was used to make a small gift for us when we left Tonga. As soon as the people from Tongatapu heard about it, they started showing up to harvest and sell the bones because of their value in the market.

We docked at O'ua and prepared to climb up the red clay hill with our gifts. As we got off the boat, we saw a group of young boys playing in the water with a long, black, hairy object. It was a horse's foreleg from an animal that had been killed and prepared for the funeral food.

After we climbed to the top of the island, the ladies stopped and put on their *ta'ovala* mats before we went to the home of the family. Sandy, being a missionary and a palangi, of course went first. She had no idea what to do, but one of the ladies motioned with her head and eyes to give her silent directions. Sandy and the two women entered the small one room house, where there were about fifteen women with frazzled hair dressed in black, wrapped in dingy old mats, sitting around the corpse singing and howling "'Oi, 'Oi, 'Oiauee" in between hymns. Sandy and her companions placed their gifts on a stack, then exited the overcrowded one-room house. We found out later that day that Sandy was supposed to kiss the corpse when she gave her offering, but Sandy was unaware and no one coached her to do so. After Sandy's group left, the women in the room went back to singing, weeping, and wailing "'Oi, 'Oi, 'Oiauee" as they had been doing all night. The wake they go through is an all-night session of singing, weeping, wailing, and eating while the men drink kava.

After almost twelve hours of their singing and weeping and wailing in the one-room house, they carried the bedridden wife of the deceased from a nearby house to the wake room. Now everyone really started wailing at the top of their lungs. After they took her out, some men came to the door with a litter of tree branches and bark to carry the body to the graveyard. Seven ministers from the Church of Tonga in Ha'afeva marched by, dressed in long black tail coats and matching pants and white shirts. They didn't visit the family or show any personal interest in them. They had come from Ha'afeva because the minister in O'ua apparently didn't have the authority to do funerals. The really sad thing was that the mourning family didn't have any money to speak of, but they had to pay the ministers, split up the offerings among them, and give them a lot of the food that had been prepared. It was a pretty profitable day for the ministers. It was most unusual to get seven at one time, and our Church members commented on the greed of bringing so many to share in distributing the offerings.

We all followed the body through the woods to the cemetery where it was to be buried. It was a spot overlooking the ocean—a very beautiful setting for the morning of the resurrection.

The seven ministers stood on an incline at the back of the cemetery and took turns reading from a book of funeral prayers. One prayer they read used the text from First Corinthians fifteen that deals with the glory of the moon, sun, and stars, but, strangely, they never explained what it meant. They never spoke of the three kingdoms of glory that they represented or anything about a plan of eternal life. I wanted so badly to stand when they were finished and bear testimony to the people of the true meaning of the scripture and how it related to the funeral.

After the brief graveside ceremony, we all marched back to the house and watched while they distributed baskets of raw horse and pig meat to every family in the village. Because of my calling as district president, we were given one of the first. The amount of meat was determined by family size— no one plays favorites at Tongan funerals, though rank and symbolism do have roles. For example, we were given the back of a pig because of my status as district president.

We ate some of the horse meat after it was cooked that night. It tasted like beef, not chicken, and because they boiled it, it was pretty tough. I can't say that it would be my first choice for dinner. I told Sandy that in the MTC for my first mission we were told as a joke never to holler "whoa" when eating horse meat as you might choke to death. So be cautious. We gave most of our meat away to the local members.

We learned a bit about the Tongan inheritance process. One of our branch members had been raised by the deceased man as a *pusiaki*, a kind of informally adopted child that's very common among Tongans, especially when a couple can't have children of their own. Our branch member was the only child raised by the deceased man and his wife, and he had lived with and cared for them as they aged. Generally, Tongan law gives the wife the right to remain on her husband's property until her death, when the property then passes to the oldest son. Since this couple had no children, it became more complicated. Even if a will had existed, it was possible that the pusiaki raised by the couple would not end up with their property. The government had to decide whether the adopted child would possess the property or it would be returned to a member of the bloodline family. It was not resolved before we completed our mission.

Valoa hadn't anchored the boat in a good place, and when the tide went out, the boat was beached on a sand bar. We had to wait at the Church building until 12:30 a.m., when the high tide returned, before we could go back home—almost twelve hours from the time we left Ha'afeva.

Coming home in the dark was slower than usual, but it was a beautiful moonlit night with a soft breeze and a clear sky. It was absolutely wonderful. Explaining the beauty of the sky that night is almost impossible. Oh, the majesty and wonder of the Lord's creations! We could see the Milky Way and the Southern Cross. The moon shone brightly, its light shimmering across the ocean's surface. The sky was full of twinkling stars. The atmosphere created a dreamy tranquil quietude and after a long and eventful day, it was like floating in the air as we sailed home.

Historic Leadership Training by an Apostle

---◆---

Most of you are in possession of your copies [of the Church Handbook of Instructions]. Read them. Understand their contents. Follow them. As we of the First Presidency meet together in our regular sessions each weekday, we must, of necessity, deal with and correct errors which are made by Church leaders in administering the affairs of the Church. Most of these errors could be avoided if such leaders were familiar with the handbook and followed the policies and procedures outlined therein.

President Thomas S. Monson, "Opening Remarks," 2010 Worldwide Leadership Training Meeting, 2010

We received our mail from the boat one day and included was a letter from the Church's Area Office in New Zealand. It apologized for the fact that some of the invitees had not received their invitation to a historic meeting of Stake and District Presidents from Tonga and Samoa to be held in Apia, Samoa three days later and informed me that I was one of those invitees. Were we ever surprised! I rushed to the telephone office and called mission headquarters to confirm that I had been invited. President Kivalu had felt that I should be included and had asked the Area Presidency to consider sending me, but he hadn't been notified that they had agreed. The letter informed me that the Church would pay for my transportation, but not Sandy's. We figured that if there was only one seat available on such short notice Sandy would just stay in Tongatapu while I went to the meeting in Samoa. The mission office found room on the plane as far as Fiji, and she flew standby for the rest of the trip to Samoa. We were blessed that the inter-island boat schedule was perfect for our travel to Tongatapu for the flight.

It was a whirlwind trip. Sandy and I had enough free time in Samoa to take a tour of the island, do some exploring on our own, and do a session in the temple. The PBO very generously provided housing and a car for us to use while we were there. Because we had been so isolated in Lulunga, the first thing that we did was to go to McDonald's and get a Big Mac, fries, and a milkshake. The chocolate milkshake was a little different because it was made with very strong Samoan dark chocolate. We had a chance to visit with a missionary couple we'd befriended in the MTC. They were serving in the Apia temple. We had dinner with the temple president and his wife on Sunday night.

Samoa is a very beautiful country with a rocky, volcanic soil and lots of mountains, hills, and vegetation. It is so different from much of Tonga, which is generally flat and sandy. The Samoan houses are different from the Tongan houses. They don't have walls—just pillars with mats that they roll down if the weather is cool or wet. They also have an elected parliament instead of a king, and the family caste system is still very strong.

Sandy was able to do quite a bit of sightseeing while I was in the training meetings. She spent Saturday with the temple president's wife; Sister Mary Cook, the area president's wife; Sister Christenson, the wife of the area presidency's executive secretary; and Sister Patricia Holland. They went to the home where Robert Louis Stevenson died and the cemetery that President Monson referred to in his April 1998 talk. (Elder Thomas S. Monson, "Look to God and Live", *Ensign*, May 1998) The wife and three children of a mission president are buried there. They also drove to a rainforest and saw the ocean from the top of the mountain. Sandy said it was spectacular.

Little did I realize what great instruction was awaiting me in those meetings. Only Stake Presidents, Mission Presidents, Temple

Presidents, and District Presidents from Samoa and Tonga attended our Saturday and Sunday meetings. These meetings were historic because they brought together the leaders of Samoa and Tonga for the first time. This was a peaceful setting as compared to their earlier history when the two countries warred with each other. I felt very humbled and honored to be invited from the little Lulunga District—it was probably the smallest unit represented at the meetings. These meetings were the second of three groups of meetings that Elder Jeffrey R. Holland of the Quorum of the Twelve conducted in the South Pacific Area along with Area President, Elder Quentin L. Cook, who we learned had been one of Elder Holland's missionary companions in England. They had already been to Fiji and would go to Tahiti for their final meeting.

The principal purpose of this historic training was to introduce the new general handbooks of instruction for the Church, which had just been translated into the Samoan and Tongan languages. Much of the time was spent instructing the leaders in English about the way the handbooks are organized and giving examples of some of the sections in the handbook. Each section introduced the doctrinal basis for the instructions, explained principles of the doctrine, and listed the specific rules. Elder Holland said simply, "It has the why, what, and how for each area." Elder Dallin H. Oaks chaired the preparation of the handbook, and it followed his very logical teaching style. The following instructions were given, as reconstructed from my notes of the meeting.

The meeting began with Elder Holland telling us that faith and testimony cause leaders to do what they do, if it works for leaders, it will work for members. We should spend more time building faith and testimony and not get consumed with administration. Each leader's success will be measured by the faith and testimonies he helps develop. Elder Holland read a quote from President Hinckley that said that if he had to be a stake president or bishop again, he would put the majority of his efforts into building the spirituality of the members. He would work as hard as he could to build faith in God, Christ, and the prophets and would encourage people to read the scriptures.

This dispensation has received more gospel knowledge and blessings than any other dispensation—almost as much as all of them combined. The size of the Church makes almost everything we have now a first, because there is no precedent from the previous generations. Every prophet before this time dreamed of this dispensation and the great things that would happen in it. They kept working at what they were called to do even though they knew that their dispensation would fail because they knew that this great last dispensation would come and never again be taken from the earth.

We have got to make the Church a millennial church. Elder Holland spoke of it as being a "lean, clean, mean, millennial church." What is that? Well, there is no mention in the revelations of wards or stakes in heaven, so he thinks that the heavens will be organized around families. We have got to get the Church to look like it will in heaven, and that is the reason for the focus on the family. This is why *The Family: A Proclamation to the World* was revealed. It is to help prepare the family for living hereafter. We will continue to hear more and more about families. He said that he believes that the day will come that this proclamation will be added to the Doctrine and Covenants. It is a very important document, and we should teach from it at every opportunity. He said that life ought to be better in LDS homes than in any other home. The Church is going to become simpler, with more focus on the family and going to the temple. Being a temple recommend holder and temple attendee tells you more about a person in the Church than anything else. We need to go to the temple more because the millennial Church includes families going to the temple. This is the reason they are building more temples in more convenient places.

One interesting point that Elder Holland made but did not comment upon was that the parable of the ten virgins has more meaning to him than ever these days. He followed that statement with saying that Lucifer will be stronger and come with more force than ever.

Elder Holland also said, "The difficulties of the South Pacific can't continue. We have got to do it right." I sensed from other things that were said in the meeting that there have been a number of specific cases of immorality with high-profile leaders as well as improper use of the sacred funds of the Church. Elder Cook said that we had to get rid of the far too common idea that this is a rich American Church and make people understand that the money of the Church comes from the poor.

Three issues stemming from the culture in the islands were discussed: wearing the garments, conducting funerals, and the Word of Wisdom. The new *Handbook of Instructions* concludes the section on wearing the garment with the following statement: "Members should be guided by these principles and the Holy Spirit to answer for themselves personal questions about wearing and caring for the garment." They told us that people should not follow the tradition of big feasts at funerals and conferences if it required going into great debt or spending excessive amounts. Funerals should become more in line with Church direction.

A lengthy discussion took place about the Word of Wisdom and drinking of kava. We were told that we were not to ask anyone in a temple recommend interview whether they drank kava, only whether they obeyed the Word of Wisdom. The only specific instructions that we have are Doctrine & Covenants 89:9 and the statement that "hot drinks" means tea and coffee—the issue is whether something you do is harmful or habit-forming. This was a major change for these leaders, as they'd been following an old area presidency letter that had forbidden kava. When I became the district president in Lulunga I was told that there was a letter from the First Presidency saying that you could not drink kava. I had asked for copies from the PBO and from the mission office but no one could come up with anything. I drank kava as a missionary, and I had been curious as to what the problem was, but it was clear that any old instruction was no longer valid.

Elder Holland followed Elder Cook's instruction with a statement about customs and cultures: "I am a Latter-day Saint who also happens to be a Tongan or Samoan, etc." He quoted from Ephesians 2:19 that when we join the Church we are "no longer strangers or foreigners" but latter-day Saints. We should be Saints first and then other things. He then gave some interesting instruction on how this fits into the Word of Wisdom issue. He quoted 1 Corinthians 6:12 to illustrate that something could be lawful but not expedient. First Corinthians 10:23 added that something could be lawful yet not edify. He said that we were not going to make rules that the Lord hadn't made, but that we must look for things that edify. He read from 1 Corinthians 8:9–13 about eating meat from the altars of pagan temples. It set a

bad example and created a stumbling block for others in Church. He
said that it is the same thing with Coke—it may offend and confuse
some people who think it's wrong. He likened the cultural issues to the
early Jewish Christians who said that all converts should be circum-
cised. Christ revealed that circumcision had been done away with (see
Galatians 2:14). Just as Peter could not compel the gentiles of the
Church to live like the Jews, we can't compel the Tongans of the Church
to behave like Americans.

There was a lengthy discussion of the signs of crisis that alarm
the brethren. Elder Holland advised leaders to sit on the stand and
observe the members, looking for early warning signs in their eyes
and faces. The eye is the light of the body, so watch it and act quickly
on things that you observe. To preface this discussion he talked about
some of the changes in the handbook that outline Church disciplinary
councils. Elder Holland said that there has been too much emphasis
on excommunication and not enough on counseling and warning
people. To change this emphasis, the brethren have now established
what is known as "formal probation" to go along with the informal
probation that bishops and stake presidents have the authority to
impose as judges in Israel. He said that the Lord would not bring a
penalty upon the earth without first giving a warning. This is a good
example for Church leaders. The signs of crisis, or "hot buttons," as
he called them, that get the Brethren more upset than anything else are
apostasy, immorality, and financial abuse. He spoke of the apostasy in
terms of disloyalty and pride. He referred to 1 Samuel 15, where Saul
was commanded to destroy both people and the animals but preserved
some of the animals for sacrifice. When he did this, he was saying, in
effect, "I know better than you do, Lord." He also spoke of Moses
striking the rock to bring forth water. When the people complained,
Moses told them he was sorry that he had to do this. The Lord rebuked
him because he took credit for the miracle and did not recognize the
Lord. Moses forgot who gave the water, and for this was not allowed
to go into the Promised Land.

On the subject of morality, Elder Holland warned that playing
with fire would get you burned. He then spent a lot of time counseling
us about not being alone with a woman to counsel her, whether at the

Church building or at her home. You should always have someone outside your door, even your wife, if necessary. He then stated that financial abuse devastated President Hinckley more than anything else. He told of the widow's mite that President Hinckley kept on his desk to remind him of where the money of the Church really came from—the poor and the widows. The funds of the Church truly are sacred.

The main issue that concerned President Hinckley was retention. The Brethren fear meeting with the Prophet because they know that he will ask about it. President Hinckley said once that as he lies in the casket during his funeral, he will rise up and ask the people, "How are we doing with retention?"

Elder Holland spent time talking about the importance of stake presidents and how they should not push so much of their priesthood responsibility down to the busy bishops of the Church. He talked about how stake presidents would now have more input about missionary work in their stakes, including missionary transfers. He said that President Hinckley feels that the Church can run well as it grows as long as it has strong stake presidents.

Some short but powerful words were said about the sisters of the Church. Elder Holland said, "The women of the Church are remarkable." He said that a quote from *The Gathering of Zion* might have said it best when talking about the Mormon pioneers: The men were great, but the "women were incredible." (Wallace Stegner, *The Gathering of Zion*, McGraw-Hill, 1971. 13) The leaders in the kingdom are blessed because of the women in their lives.

In the latter part of the meeting on Sunday morning, Elder Holland gave scriptural instruction. He took 1 Nephi 1 and had various people read verses 5, 6–9, 11, and 12. He then asked us to think about how this related to the Joseph Smith experience. If you read it, you will see that Lehi went forth to pray and had a vision of God the Father and Jesus Christ. A book was given to him, and he read various warnings that he then took to the people, who rejected and tried to kill him. It was a very enlightening exercise. He then had us read other scriptures in 1 Nephi and taught us how one purpose of the Book of Mormon was to teach people about revelation. He said that you must read it and learn to believe in revelation and that you can't join the Church until you do. The Book of Mormon uses dreams, visions, prophecies, books, scriptures, and records to teach about revelation. It also teaches us about choices and opposition.

One of Elder Holland's final points came from a sports metaphor. In sports, no one wants to join a team that's definitely going to lose. Though it's already known that the devil's team is going to lose, people continue to join it. Even some people on the winning team want to change jerseys and play for the losers. He couldn't understand why anyone would want to be with the losing team.

This trip and meeting were one of the highlights of our mission. Being called to the little village of Ha'afeva, Tonga, we did not envision being able to travel to another country and participate in special leadership training by an apostle. I learned much and felt the powerful spirit of the meeting. My life will never be the same. When you accept the call as a missionary it is hard to envision the great blessings that await you. We were blessed to enjoy many instructions from General Authorities.

A Missionary Transfer

❖

*I have faith and confidence that every missionary is called
by revelation . . . I am always happy when the missionary
says, "I am in your hands, in the hands of the Lord, from
this moment forward, and I will go where he sends me."*

President Spencer W. Kimball, *The Teachings of
Spencer W. Kimball,* Bookcraft, Inc. 1982, 563

We got up at 4 a.m. on Monday to return to Tonga. We ran a
few errands in Nuku'alofa after we arrived, and before we
got on the boat to Ha'afeva we had a meeting with President Kivalu
that made our day feel even longer. President Kivalu called us into
his office and told us that he was transferring us to Niue, an island
nation almost 400 miles to the east of the mission headquarters in
Nuku'alofa, Tonga. We went into a state of shock and sorrow—we
almost started wailing 'Oi, 'Oi, 'Oiauee!" There were so many things
in Ha'afeva that still needed to be done—we had so many plans! They
say that when you're called to a position you should be prepared to be
released the next day, but that is easier said than done. We hoped the
new district president would be able to implement some of our plans
and that things would continue progressing. We were told we would
probably leave the next week.

After the last Lulunga District conference a rumor had spread
that we were going to be transferred because President Kivalu, in his

closing remarks, commented that we wouldn't be here very long. We'd figured he'd meant that the mission was a short amount of time, but I guess the people were more perceptive than we were. President Kivalu had already planned the transfer and received approval from Elder Halverson, of the Area Presidency.

Our last boat ride to Ha'afeva was overcrowded with people and cargo, so I tried to sleep sitting up. There really wasn't room to lie down. Cargo was all over the area where passengers normally sit, so even the sitting room was limited. We were sitting on some lumber that was only marginally comfortable. We arrived home and got to sleep about 3:30 a.m. Needless to say, it was a long day.

We didn't know it beforehand, but the lumber and other building materials on the boat were being sent to build a chapel in Kotu. The Kotu Branch was currently meeting in the tiny house of a member in which the Elders also slept. There were cracks in the walls big enough to stick your hand through, and the roof leaked a lot. There would also be a new two-room house built for the Elders on the Church property. This was good news to make our departure a little sweeter.

When we got back to Ha'afeva we learned from a woman who belonged to another church that someone had spread the word about our transfer and that there was a Tongan couple from the States coming. There are no secrets in Tonga. The coconut wireless is very effective.

In our new assignment in Niue, we would represent President Kivalu and the mission. We were to help the branch presidents and district president get organized and resolve various issues. We assumed the assignment of the Tongan-American couple coming to Ha'afeva would be to serve as district president. We were hopeful that we would have a chance to meet them and orient them about the Lulunga District's current issues and the plans we had to solve them, but unfortunately that never happened.

Before we left for Niue, we met with the missionary couple that had been there from October to March the previous year. They said the people were very generous and loving with missionaries but not with their own people and that they would listen to a missionary couple better than one of their own.

Our New Home

Niue (pronounced "nee-oo-ay") is a sparkling, beautiful coral atoll island. It is one of the largest coral atolls in the world. It is referred to in the South Pacific as "the rock of Polynesia" or simply as "the rock." The island is 17 miles long and 10 miles wide at its widest point. It has a total area of 100 square miles—about the size of Washington, DC. It sits out in the middle of the ocean with nothing else to be seen anywhere around, which in some ways made us feel more isolated than ever. In Ha'afeva, we knew there was life a boat ride away. Here there was nothing. The closest island is the northern island group of Vava'u, Tonga which is 270 miles to the west. People had to fly to go anywhere. It was hotter than Hades, and a smelly, sweaty body was the order of the day and night. We had none of the nice ocean breezes like we'd had in the Lulunga area, so we resurrected a fan from a closet. It helped some.

On the positive side, we found we could get almost any basic food we might want. There was a butcher's shop that sold hamburger and another place that had cheese, sour cream, and cream cheese. They had lots of local watermelons and other fruits and vegetables imported from New Zealand that you could buy, and there was also a little famers' market on Friday mornings. They even had some delicious New Zealand ice cream. We were hopeful that the pounds we'd lost with the more restrictive diet in Ha'afeva wouldn't find their way back.

The house, located in the capital city of Alofi, was nice but not great. Unlike in Ha'afeva, it was located on a well-paved asphalt thoroughfare, though it was still on the fenced-in Church property. They had recently repainted all the rooms a turquoise blue. It looked like what you might expect to see in Mexico on the outside of a house. The furniture was very old. We had helped design the house in Ha'afeva, so it was built to fit our needs, and most of the furnishings were new and very nice. We arrived in Niue to find that the oven and stove weren't working. Though the district president suggested that we cook on the Church stove, we mostly used our can opener and had cold food until they were fixed. We also had a nice refrigerator as well as a box freezer, a conventional washer, and a clothes line. We now had electricity all the time, a bathroom with hot water, and 3 small bedrooms, although one was considered an office. We also had fax and copy machines.

We were also the Niue distribution center, so if anyone wanted to buy garments, books, or other Church materials, they came to us and ordered them. We faxed the order to the PBO, and they sent it from Tonga on the next plane. We had a garage, but our van wouldn't fit inside it. There was also a big storage house for all PBO supplies.

At least there were no pigs running around here—they were all penned up. We had a few stray chickens in the yard, more ants than I have ever seen, standard large size roaches and large land crabs known as a "coconut crabs" that we would see running across the road or in the yard.

We were happy to find that Alofi had a water system that piped water to our house. The rainwater cistern was only for emergency use. We were even more amazed at where this water came from. Because Niue is a giant coral reef, there is actually seawater underneath it. Rainwater seeps through the soil to this underground lagoon, but because freshwater is less dense than saltwater, it actually floats. The water that was piped into the homes came from this freshwater layer that forms underneath the island.

We reflected that this transfer was easy compared to the early pioneer Saints that had just gotten settled, planted their crops and then were asked to load everything into a wagon again and move to a drier, unsettled place and start over. We reminded ourselves that our simple transfer was not reason to grumble or complain.

Believe it or not, we knew we would miss our ocean trips. When you spend a lot of time in, around, and on the ocean you develop a love affair with it. We would definitely miss our friends in Ha'afeva, especially the children. Hopefully we influenced some of them for good that will be reflected in their later lives. Although we could count the good things that had been accomplished, it was still difficult to leave with so many loose ends still dangling. We had really gotten into a rhythm and were moving ahead quickly.

The best part of the transfer was that we did not get new companions.

A New Culture

> *. . . couples leave comfortable homes, grandchildren, and recreation, often multiple times, for distant parts of the world to live under the most humble circumstances. A few learn a foreign language; many experience vastly different cultures, accepting challenges they are not sure they can cope with. Yet these . . . couples return from service given at great personal sacrifice, thanking the Lord for the privilege. There is nothing like it in the world.*

Elder Richard G. Scott, "The Power of Correct Principles," *Ensign*, May 1993, 32

While major changes took place in Niue with the coming of Christian missionaries, other changes happened when the island was annexed by New Zealand in 1961. The isolation of Niue began to decline with the visits of ocean liners like the Tofua that circled the South Pacific islands on a monthly basis in the late 1950s and early 1960s. The population of the island peaked at approximately 5,000 but with the development of an airport in 1971 and the granting of New Zealand citizenship to Niueans a massive outward migration began and the current population has now dipped to less than 1800. Today, however, there are approximately 15,000 Niueans living in New Zealand.

With all of these changes, the old culture has been swallowed up by the advancing technology influence of New Zealand. The dress today is typical of New Zealand, and a significant part of the diet comes from imported sources. I found that the traditional Polynesian sharing had declined significantly and Niueans had become selfish like the people of developed countries. It was a great contrast with the isolated Ha'afeva area where we first served and much of the old culture of Tonga was preserved.

We arrived in Niue just before Christmas, so we attended parties with lots of good food and performances by some of the local youth. They don't have a distinctive Niuean style of dancing like they do in Tonga—they instead danced various Polynesian dances. We learned that they don't have a dance culture of their own. When the London Missionary Society (LMS) was the governing body of the country, they actually used to beat people who would sing or dance Niuean songs and dances. As a result, modern Niuean dances are a conglomerate of other Polynesian dances.

Feasts and Food Handling

Not long after our transfer from Tonga, we attended our first Niuean feast in Lakepa. It was a rude awakening to the vast differences between these two South Pacific cultures. In contrast to feasts in Tonga, where we frequently sat on the ground cross-legged, in Niue we sat at picnic tables with benches. That was only the beginning. As is traditional in Niue, a prayer was given by a local minister before the feasting took place. Almost before the minister had said "Amen," the people were grabbing food off the tables and placing it in a basket or other container they'd brought with them. We first thought the people were rude, but one of the members noticed we hadn't brought a basket and told us what was taking place. We learned that it's a custom of the country and decided that we'd better get used to it. While Tongans would have been taking a chicken leg to eat, the Niueans were placing the whole cooked chickens or six-pound cans of corned beef in their baskets to take home. After everyone had chosen the food they'd take home, they ate what was left on the table. Leftovers suddenly took on new meaning. The trick, we learned, was to stake out your table, figure what you wanted to take home, and grab it for your basket as soon as the prayer was over.

The next feast we attended was a pot-luck and the worst yet for rudeness and crowding while trying to get the food. I finally just settled for a few things and stepped out of the fray. It was amazing to see people fill plates and baskets to take home while they were eating. I thought that I had figured out the system, and I took a large container to gather food to take to the Elders. The food was a little short this time, so people just filled up their plates and baskets and there was nothing left to go back to the tables to eat. I thought during the filling of my plate and jockeying for food, that I was on the New York subway. The Niueans are usually polite to visitors but I guess they had determined early that the food was short and they were not about to let anyone get more than them.

Ear Piercing and Haircutting Ceremonies

Two significant cultural events in Niue are the *hifi ulu* and the *huki teliga*. The *hifi ulu* is a coming of age ceremony for a male child in his early teens. His long hair is cut for the first time since his birth, symbolizing his passage into adulthood. The *huki teliga* ear-piercing ceremony similarly marks puberty for young women. Both these ceremonies are very important events in every Niuean family and are occasions for displaying family solidarity, wealth, and status. They often involve donating cash or gifts to the celebrants. These gifts are reciprocated by an elaborate and public presentation of feast foods. The extended family does extra work to procure sufficient quantities of pigs, fish, taro, ufi, yams, salted pork, and canned corned beef.

One Saturday morning we received a call from a member in the village of Tuapa. He said he was sorry to be so late inviting us, but could we come to his daughter's ear-piercing ceremony? We had heard the ceremony was going on and had hoped to be invited because we'd never attended one before. We had already planned to take the Elders to see the cave at the Liku Sea Track, so we did so, then hurried home, showered, and went to the ear-piercing ceremony.

As usual, we were surprised by what happened next—life as missionaries is one surprise after another. One of the uncles of the girl came up and asked me to offer the opening prayer for the ceremony. There were five chairs set up at the front of the hall. They were all covered with colorful fabric, one chair in front and the other four just behind. Obviously, the one in front was for Sonita, the girl of the day. Because I was giving the opening prayer, they asked us to come and sit in two of the chairs up front. The minister of the LMS Church in Tuapa and his wife sat in the other two chairs. After several speeches were made, they casually mentioned that I would now help the LMS minister bless Sonita and after the blessing I was to give some appropriate remarks, followed by the LMS minister. I had not been told in advance that I would be asked to do these things. Then the two of us each laid one hand on her head and the LMS minister gave one prayer in Niuean and I gave a prayer in English. Sandy was as baffled as I was. In my remarks I spoke of what the Savior had said about ears, telling people that they have ears but hear not. Though we saw one function of the ears in having them pierced, the most important role of the ear was to listen and learn from the word of the Lord. After the blessing and the remarks, some women came forward and pierced Sonita's ears, squeezing fresh lime juice on the holes afterwards.

The LMS minister and I were then taken outside the building and each asked to offer a blessing on the food that had been put into bags to be distributed. They were a little surprised when I gave my blessing in Niuean instead of English. This was not a normal prayer for blessing the food that was about to be eaten, but more of a general blessing like you might give to bless your home. Inside cookies and punch were then passed around while a woman called out the names of people who had contributed money to the celebration according to the amount that had been contributed. When each contributor came up, they were given a bag containing biscuits, cake, and candy.

While this was going on with the women, the men were lining up the taro and organizing the meat gifts. The ceremony was over by 11:00 a.m. and we waited and watched men hack up pigs, sheep, and fish until 2:30 p.m. They distributed the meat in baskets according to how much money and goods had been contributed to the family. There were twenty-five pigs, ten sheep and about fifteen very large fish. They also distributed cans of corned beef and frozen chickens. It was quite a sight to watch them use the axes and bush knives on the frozen carcasses of the animals. When they had finished, they proceeded to call out the names of the people by their piles, from the highest contributor down to the lowest.

The LMS minister and I were called first. Compared to some, Sandy and I received a fairly small amount, but more than we expected. We received five chickens, a six-pound can of corned beef, a huge whole tuna, and about eighteen taro roots. At the end of the day, we realized it had nothing to do with Sonita and her ear piercing and everything to do with payback and money. One of the Elders tried to tell us that they consider it an investment and that it has nothing to do with the person. We felt that it was a lot of show. It reconfirmed our suspicion that many Niueans needed to learn how to give without expecting anything in return.

The payback system is very strong in Niue. When a person is invited to a wedding, ear piercing, or hair-cutting ceremony, they give money and possibly help with the party. The hosts of the party keep a list of exactly how much money is given and how much time is spent helping. When someone on their list then has an event of some kind, they use their list to see how much money they were given by that person, and they give the same amount or more in return. Many just don't understand the concept of helping someone for the sake of serving them. There are people, of course, like Elder and Sister Molai, our local missionary couple, who did service and didn't expect anything in return, but they were the exception, not the rule.

Burial Custom

Our district president's 97 year-old mother died after an extended hospital stay from a broken hip. She was one of the pioneers of the Church in Niue having been part of the first baptisms into the Church in 1952 and had been a stalwart member ever since. It had only been the last few years that she hadn't been healthy enough to working out in the yard. She had requested not to be put in the freezer, but to be buried the same day she died. The family decided against that and waited two days for one of her daughters to come from New Zealand. The chapel and cultural hall were filled to overflowing, mostly with nonmembers. Sandy typed up a very nice program the likes of which they had never had in Niue to distribute to the family members. I was asked to give the closing prayer, a typical gesture to make the palangi feel good. The sad thing about the funeral was that the great plan of salvation was not preached. I prayed in English and tried to mention a little of the plan of salvation, but I didn't want to pray too long. A great opportunity was missed to discuss gospel principles with so many nonmembers. I should have been alert and encouraged the members that spoke to include the plan of salvation in their talks, but I wasn't. The burial took place, as customary in Niue and Samoa, right in district president's front yard. Everyone watched as the cement was poured to seal the grave. Many of the people then went to Gabe's, a local restaurant, for a potluck dinner provided by the family.

For the week after the funeral, groups from various Churches and organizations came by to visit the family, who were responsible for feeding their visitors. The groups, however, in traditional custom, brought money to the family, so at least feeding them wasn't a great financial burden like it was in Tonga.

In the front yard of our home there was a grave and a marker. It was a strange feeling to see that in our front yard because it was the grave of a missionary, a Sister Wyatt who became sick and died in 1962 while serving a mission with her husband in Niue. Her remains were exhumed in 1966 and returned to America, but the marker remained in place as a monument to her faithful service.

A Niuean Wedding—Almost

We had the opportunity to attend one wedding during our six months on Niue. It was something new and different and a good way to learn about the culture. The wedding itself was held at our Church, followed by a reception at the home of the groom's aunt, who was a cabinet minister in the Niue parliament and was next in authority to the premier. She lived in a very nice, roomy house provided by the government and was an active member of the Church. Susianna, the Tongan bride, wore a traditional Tongan outfit for the wedding, which was quite remarkable to most of the Niueans there. The opening song was in Tongan, so basically only the Tongan guests sang. Wedding advice was given mostly in Niuean, though some of it was repeated in English. The wedding ceremony itself, including signing the government registry books, was done in English, as were the other songs. Most of the people there were not members, and both a Catholic priest and the Seventh-day Adventist minister attended.

The reception featured lots of food, of course, and some dancing and singing afterwards. The most unusual thing to us was that between dances and songs, different families would come forward and lay several layers of lengthy, six-foot wide fabric across the laps of the bride and groom and stand at the end of the fabric and make wishes and give advice while throwing money on the fabric. No real gifts were given, only lots of money. The bride's Tongan aunt used a tapa cloth instead of fabric for her gift.

Food and Visits to New Zealand

Niue is a protectorate of New Zealand, so lots of people travel back and forth. It is a tradition when going to New Zealand that Niueans bring Niuean food with them regardless of the cost, so they stay up a good part of the night before they leave cooking food in umus to take in a big cooler to their family and friends. When people return from New Zealand, they are expected to bring back heaps of Kentucky Fried Chicken and Big Macs. It appeared to us that people were always anxious to go to the airport because they wanted to be first to get some chicken or Big Mac.

What's for Lunch?

In addition to the fruit on the trees and the fish in the sea, there were many other good natural food sources on the island. There were pigs and chickens, both wild and domestic. While Niueans eat many New Zealand dishes, they love their locally grown food. A wonderful meal could be had from the *uga* (oon-ga), the seemingly ubiquitous coco-nut-eating land crabs. It is a large crab. It can grow as big as two feet long. It is unusual in that it eats coconuts. It climbs up the coconut tree backwards, snips off a coconut with its pinchers, climbs back down, and takes the coconut apart with its powerful claws, which takes a great amount of strength. They taste like king crab, only sweeter because of their coconut diet.

Niueans also enjoyed the small *Kalahimus* land crabs, though you need a lot of them to make a good meal. They live in the coral rock and make themselves a nuisance when it rains by seeking shelter wherever they can find it. We found them all over our little quarters after rainstorms, usually in our shoes and bedding.

One of the unusual seasonal foods was the *Kaloama*, a sardine-like fish that visit Niue's shores in February. Fishermen chase them into shallow reef areas which are then closed off, and all the nearby villagers then catch them using nets, fishing lines and spears.

They also ate *peka*, a three-foot wing spread fruit bat also known as the flying fox. They dwell in caves and trees. December is peka hunting season, and we frequently heard gunshots around Christmas. As we drove to the various villages at night, we saw men along the roadside with shotguns hunting peka. The hunters are required to stay on the road—going into the forest to hunt is illegal. At one meal with some members Sandy was adventurous and ate some bat meat. It was cooked whole in banana leaves, and when she opened the leaves there were two little eyes peering out at her. I had eaten peka as a young missionary in Tonga but had never acquired a taste for it.

The Takai

One Saturday morning in January a young lady came bounding up the front stairs, opened the front door, and handed us an invitation addressed to the "Head of the LDS mission and good lady." It was for the *Takai*. Every January to celebrate the New Year, the people in Alofi decorate their cars, trucks, and motorcycles and drive the circumference of the entire island, going through every village, honking their horns, and throwing candy out the windows to kids. We gathered up the Elders and went with them. We didn't know about the candy part, so we felt a little silly just honking and waving, but we did it anyway. We figured it would take maybe an hour or two, but it was three and a half hours before we arrived home. It was certainly a long, slow, and unusual way to welcome in the New Year—another unique cultural experience.

Moving Parked Cars

Whenever people park their cars in the market area they leave their keys in their cars so if the car is in the way someone can move it. One day we went to the post office and were only gone for a few minutes. When we came back, there were two cars parked behind us and a motorcycle on the side of us. We were blocked in! The car closest behind us was a police car. We waited for a few minutes and then I got out of the car and moved the police car. We were then able to leave. Can you imagine doing that in America? This was a clear demonstration that they didn't have any car thefts in the country.

Niuean Pride

While talking with District President Haioti one evening we learned a little about the pride of the Niuean Saints. In 1990 a large hurricane hit the island. The Church was the first to send in assistance, but they made sure that it went to the neediest people even if they were not members of the Church. The members of the LMS Church got a lot of the help even though they have always been critical of the Church and have rejected our missionary effort, even to the extent of not letting missionaries tract in some of the villages. Giving needed assistance to LMS members who had persecuted the Church angered some Niuean LDS church members so much that they would not accept the assistance from the Church, especially when the Church said that they should do some service to get the items. They told the Church to go to hell. This was another demonstration of the Niueans being a very proud people.

Scope of Missionary Activities

Serving a mission gives retired people a chance to use their talents and gifts again. They discover that they are truly needed, and as a consequence they find a powerful new sense of direction in life. They joyfully lose themselves in new experiences and opportunities for growth. The reward for those who serve is often renewed health and energy. When they go home, they are filled with the rich spirit of missionary work and a great love for the people they have served.

Elder David B. Haight, "Couple Missionaries—'A Wonderful Resource,'" *Ensign*, Feb 1996, 6–12

Our missionary role in Niue was very different from our role in Ha'afeva. President Kivalu specifically asked us to work with the missionaries to improve the proselyting efforts in the country. He also called me to be a counselor in the Niue District Presidency instead of his representative. Our full-time missionaries originally included two full-time Elders and a local missionary couple, Elder and Sister Molai. I had served with the grandfather of one of the Elder's in the Vava'u District Presidency during my first mission to Tonga. Two other full-time Elders were added later. Two of our biggest missionary successes were the Open House and the Songfest held in conjunction with our district conferences.

Niue District Activities

The Niue District had 220 members, three cinderblock chapels, and four branches: Alofi, Niue South, Niue North, and Lakepa-Liku. I was now a counselor in the District Presidency with responsibility for the youth programs, so I instituted a monthly Friday night youth dance and another Friday night for activities held at the various chapels to help build unity among youth and keep them active. I also hoped that it would serve as a missionary tool for their friends. I also instituted a monthly youth fireside held on a Sunday evenings. We had four firesides while we were there, and the subjects were thoughts, standards, member missionary work, and avoiding evil. The youth that attended always enjoyed these firesides, especially when they featured a video.

With the aid of our laptop computer, we put together a district calendar, something they had never had before. It contained the same items found in most stake calendars in the Church, as well as a spiritual thought at the top of each page that reflected that month's district council theme.

I attended all the district presidency and district council meetings, but many were not well attended, and they usually started very late. Unlike in Tonga, they seldom prepared an agenda for the meeting. I always prepared one just in case, and it was almost always the one we used. Sometime in the history of Tonga, the principle of preparing an agenda was taught so well that it became automatic. In fact, some of the agendas in Tonga exceeded what I was accustomed to in my home stake and ward. The Tongans make an art form of the agenda. I did the best I could in Niue. I tried to schedule myself to give instruction from the General Handbook of Instructions because I knew that they would not undertake this learning by themselves. It was hard to sit back and not take the lead after serving as the District President of Lulunga.

One of the successful initiatives was a planned temple trip to Samoa. This was a major financial commitment as it would cost over $400 per person. We tried to plan this so that we would attend with them on our way home from our mission but were not able to do so because the temple was closed for maintenance. The members attended after we returned home. We were happy to see the effort fulfilled in a successful temple trip.

Missionary Meetings

Every Monday morning we had a missionary meeting at our home in Alofi. These meetings were some of the highlights of our mission. I viewed them as reporting, planning, and practicing meetings. We talked about the activities of the previous week and discussed how we could improve. We also practiced presenting the missionary lessons in Niuean. Each week, one companionship was assigned to present a lesson to the other missionaries in Niuean. This not only helped us all learn the language but significantly improved our teaching skills. Unfortunately, we did not get a lot of practice teaching discussions to investigators. We also spent time bearing testimonies and planning our open house, songfest, and missionary survey activities. These meeting were generally very spiritually uplifting and gave us a boost going forward that week.

Molai Mission Call

One day there was a heap of mail in our mailbox. We were surprised— it wasn't even mail day. As we looked through it, we saw that it was all addressed to the Lakepa-Liku branch. Included in the mail was the November 1997 mission call of Elder and Sister Molai and the notification to the branch president thereof. It was 1999, and they had been serving for almost a year. Apparently, the rent on the branch post office box hadn't been paid for over a year, so the box had been cancelled, and the mail had been held somewhere. The Molais had never received an official, written call; they'd just been informed by the mission president and began serving. It was nice to now have an official letter from the prophet. The call stated that they were to live at home, not attend the MTC, and continue in their branch and district callings unless that interfered with their missionary work.

Service Project

One week the full-time missionaries did a service project of preparing for and painting the National Women's Hall. Sandy and I, the four

Elders, and the Molais worked from 8:00 a.m. to 4:00 p.m. wiping down walls, cleaning windows, and sanding door frames. Sandy and Sister Molai left at 1:30 p.m. to make dinner. We got the undercoat of paint on the walls, and then the members of the district came and finished painting with us. The New Zealand High Commission provided the materials for the job. It was a very productive day of service, and we raised awareness of our desire to serve the community. I assume that we were no different than other senior missionaries in constantly looking for ways to serve the community and raise awareness of the Church.

Niue Church Distribution Center

One activity we didn't anticipate when we came to Niue was our assignment to handle Church distribution items. This expanded after we arrived to include garments and temple clothing. We originally handled all distribution orders by way of our fax machine, but when we expanded we bought a four-drawer dresser for storing the temple clothes. When the First Presidency announced that each temple recommend holder should have their own set of temple clothes, they also offered a tremendous discount on them. The people of Niue don't go to the temple very often because it requires expensive travel to Samoa or New Zealand, so not many of them purchased their own temple clothing. We were thankful that we had this expanded activity to help them.

TV and Radio Ads

We sought to have church public service announcements placed on TV and radio in Niue. The stations weren't big, but they did a good job. We made contact with the Church Public Affairs Office in the South Pacific and asked what material they could supply. We had only thought about nice TV spots on the family, but they reminded us that *Music and Spoken Word* is available on CD for radio as well as DVD for TV.

Our discussions with the local radio and TV executives were not as fruitful as we'd hoped. They told us that they were under contract with New Zealand TV Company and they could only play what they

were sent or what was actually produced in Niue. We tried to get the
Music and The Spoken Word on radio and on TV through New Zealand.
We even prepared a proposal and tried to get their Board to approve
it, but we were never successful. I believe that if we'd only had to
work through the Niuean stations we would have succeeded. There are
bureaucratic barriers to good things going forward in some countries,
especially when the name of the Church is attached.

Special Missionary Survey

We developed a plan to go to each village and do a survey of every
household. We first acquired maps of each village and the names of
all the adults in them from the government. We made a list of questions that would help people think about the Church, such as, "Do you
know that Mormons do not worship Joseph Smith?" and "Have you
ever heard of The Church of Jesus Christ of Latter-day Saints?" When
we suggested doing the survey, the missionaries and members agreed
only reluctantly because many of the villages around the island had
prohibited missionaries from tracting.

Our first survey was in the village of Lakepa, where Elder and
Sister Molai lived. It had been raining all night, but we decided we
would go anyway and test our faith, so we picked up the Elders and
went. We sang a song, said a prayer, and waited for about twenty
minutes, but it still continued to rain heavily. Like many heavy rains in
the islands it came by the bucket full. We wondered if maybe it wasn't
the right time to do the survey. We decided to each do one survey on
our own after the rain subsided and report back on Monday as to how
it went. Sandy and I visited one active and two less-active members,
but no one was home. It was a disappointing first day, but we resolved
to try again.

The next week we surveyed the villages of Avatele and Tamakautonga with the Elders, and this time it was a good experience. The
Elders took one side of the village road and Sandy and I took the
other. The Elders even found one man in Avatele who appeared to
have some interest. Elder Ikakoula said afterward that it was a very
good experience for him because he felt fluent in Niuean for the first
time. Our biggest problem was the same one faced in most of the

rest of the world: people are gone to work during the day. In Niue, if they're not working in the main village of Alofi they're in the bush working in their gardens. With the village maps from the government, we were able to identify which houses had nobody home so that we could go back later.

After our experience with the first two villages, we decided to visit the next villages in the late afternoon. We had a little more success than the Elders because it was unique to have palangi knock on a door in the outer villages. It's unusual for senior couples to tract in any mission—they specifically told us in the MTC that we weren't expected to do it—so we were unique in Niuean missionary work.

The Molais had a great fear of the missionaries being banned from tracting in the villages. They told us that Tamakautonga would be a very difficult village that we should perhaps avoid, but we had some very good visits there and got seven or eight homes to fill out our survey. The people learned some things about the Church from it, and we learned some of their names and made some ties with the community. When we got to the end of the village and met up with the Elders. They told us that the people in the first house they'd visited had seen us go to the home across the road from them and told the Elders that the last time someone from the Church had visited that home, an old man had chased them away with a bush knife. It's a good thing we didn't know that before we started.

In Avatele we had people talk to us but refuse to fill out the survey. In Tamakautonga, the people were friendly, and only one family hid from us. It was also a good opportunity to practice the language since many of the people in the outer villages were not as comfortable with English, though they do fairly well.

Based on these two successes, we decided to go to the village of Hakupu, which we were told would give us the greatest trouble. Everyone talked about how the village had thrown stones at the Elders a number of years before. While the stoning was quite some time ago and no one had been hurt, their reputation had stayed with them. We went and tested the water, and while we didn't have a lot of success, we were not stoned. The first family that the Elders visited told them that it had been many years since the Mormons had tracted in the village.

While our success with the survey was hard to measure, it did get us before the people in every village in the country and hopefully gave the Church more recognition. It also provided the full-time Elders a meaningful activity and the follow-up helped to fill their future schedule.

Member Transportation—Taxi Service

We were informed upon our arrival in Niue that one of the most important roles we would fulfill was transporting members to Church in the mission van. Although this was contrary to the general missionary rules, it had been done for at least ten years. It seems that a number of years ago the Church sold a couple of small, wooden chapels because of the decline in membership in the villages they served. To pacify the members, someone told them the Church would provide transportation for them to other chapels. This was never memorialized in writing, so there had always been a question about the appropriateness, but we spent quite a bit of time every Sunday transporting people to and from their regular meetings and to occasional firesides. We also transported people to various social activities, especially the weekend youth activities and dances. We also picked up individuals for home-study seminary and institute on Thursdays and Niue South Branch Relief Society homemaking meetings once a month. Both of our mission vans were used primarily for these purposes.

Welfare Visits

One night a woman from our branch knocked on our door and invited Sandy to come with their branch to do their welfare visits. Sandy had no clue what that would be, but agreed to go. As they would go into a member's house, the woman of the house would have all her food storage stacked in one place for all of them to see. If there was a special treat included with the supplies that looked good to one of the visiting sisters, she would take it. It was another example of the Polynesian culture of not being selfish. They came home with granola bars, chips, candy, and more. The women who were doing the visiting also took everyone else to their homes to see their food storage. Apparently they have done this once a month for a while. They gave a suggested list once a month of what to buy. Some of the supplies were pretty meager. It was uplifting to us to see how these members strove to follow the direction of the Church leaders using their own original approach.

Translation Activities with Niuean Language

◆

For it shall come to pass in that day, that every man shall
hear the fullness of the gospel in his own tongue, and in
his own language, through those who are ordained unto
this power, by the administration of the Comforter, shed
forth upon them for the revelation of Jesus Christ.

Doctrine and Covenants 90:11

We knew that we would have to learn a new language with our transfer, but we were very surprised when we were asked to help translate various documents from English to Niuean. Every month, the Church paid a local Niuean member to translate the visiting teaching and First Presidency messages. This translation would be hand written and mailed to Australia, where it would be typed up and mailed back to Niue for corrections. The corrections were noted and the document was again sent to Australia. We came to the mission field with a laptop computer, so we got Sandy to type the hand written information instead. Once she had the typing corrections completed in Niue, we emailed it to Australia for printing. This shortened the turnaround time by more than two weeks. Typing documents in Niuean, plus our daily translation of the Niuean Book of Mormon like we did with Tongan in Ha'afeva, accelerated Sandy's learning of Niuean much faster than my own.

We had some concerns about what was and wasn't getting

translated, and so we contacted the Director of Church Translation in Australia. He was excited that someone on location could give him some input. The Area Presidency has most of the say about what takes place in translation, but it appeared that they hadn't shown much interest in Niue. We thought that it would be best to spend the energy on the Book of Mormon and not a lot of administration manuals. The then-current translation of the Book of Mormon in Niuean was only a partial translation of certain important parts, which is what the Church usually does with languages that only have limited use in a small population.

When we were eating breakfast one morning, a thought came to me about the translation. After the Church manuals are translated, they are sent to Salt Lake to be printed. There was a minimum number that have to be printed—several hundred, though I wasn't sure exactly how many—and the only place to use them was Niue. It seemed to be a waste of the widow's mite. There were still members in Niue who couldn't read English well enough to understand a lesson, but most branches had teachers who were quite capable of teaching from an English manual. I suggested via email that they photocopy a specific number of manuals, make a nice cover for them, bind them, and send them to Niue. It seemed to be a lot more economical that way. Victor Cave, who was in charge of all translations for the South Pacific, agreed and asked us to find out for sure what the official language of the island was. The Area Presidency was reviewing whether the Book of Mormon should be translated fully. We didn't want to see all translation stopped, but we knew there had to be a way to save money. When we left the mission field, no final decision had been made.

As we read and translated the Niuean Book of Mormon each day for language study, we would sometimes find translation errors. Whole sentences were sometimes left out, and other times it was just plain wrong, like a reference in Third Nephi to *idolatry* that was translated in Niuean as *adultery*.

One week we asked the branch president why they conducted the meeting in Niuean but said the sacrament prayers in English. He said he understood that they were not to use the Niuean card because of some translation errors. We asked the District President about it and he suggested that Sandy type it up the way it was translated in the Book of Mormon, which is correct. She did so and we laminated the cards. I handed them out at the branch presidency meeting, which stimulated quite a bit of discussion. The problem was the word used for water, which we had to add ourselves because the Book of Mormon uses the word *wine*. We'd used the word *vai*, which was used in the Niuean *Family Handbook* section on ordinances, but the old sacrament prayer cards used the word *maga vai*. Our search of the current Niuean to English dictionary found many different types of water and that *maga vai* means only freshwater, which we concluded was not the correct word to use. We learned that translating correctly is much harder than we thought, even for simple words like *water*.

The Open House — An Unfamiliar Concept

$$\diamondsuit$$

This impression weighed upon me that the Church is at point in its growth and maturing when we are at last ready to move forward in a major way. We have paused on some plateaus long enough. Think, brothers and sisters, of having a "Bring a Family to Church" week, open houses, and special missionary firesides.

President Spencer W. Kimball, New Mission
Presidents Seminar, June 22, 1979

On March 15, 1999, almost 20 years after President Kimball's request to hold open houses, we held a missionary open house in conjunction with the district conference visit of President and Sister Kivalu and his first counselor.

We advertised the open house on the radio for three days. We thought we'd paid for three announcements, but they announced it three times a day for three days—a real bargain. We also put a little ad on the national email system in Niue, one day a week for two weeks. We hand delivered personalized invitations to every government official, including the High Commissioner from New Zealand, the Premier, all the National Assembly, ministers of every Church and each village council chairman. We also made invitations for the members to give to their friends. Each card had a blank space for the member to fill in their friends' names. Each of these invitations to government officials was for the pre-open house reception as well as for the open house itself. Finally we made half-page general invitations for each member and missionary to pass out to anyone they met or visited.

The afternoon before the open house, the TV stations called and asked if they could interview me about the open house and what we expected to accomplish. The term *open house* was new to them, and many people had been asking us what it meant. This was actually helpful because people came out of curiosity.

We had done a lot but all the little things that bring it together yet remained. We tried not to build our hopes too high that it would be an overwhelming success, but it was hard not to be excited. We knew that we would have a hundred members, but the question was how many of their friends and other invitees would come. The open house program was to start with a pre-open house at 6:30 p.m. for all the especially invited dignitaries of Niue to meet with President Kivalu before the main activity at 7:00 p.m. This was something new here, so we were curious as to how well it would turn out.

The Lord touched the people's hearts. The first bus load of people arrived a half-hour early, and they just kept coming. Even some of the ministers from other Churches came for a while. It was also election week, so most of the candidates showed up to shake hands and let people see their presence. It became the big event on the island—everyone wanted to be there. We literally had standing room only, and there were probably forty people standing outside because there were no chairs. People loved the food, and of course carried home plates of goodies in true Niuean style.

The open house program started in the cultural hall with the prelude music "Called to Serve" sung by us six full-time missionaries. We sang the first verse three times, once each in English, Tongan, and Niuean. We then had a congregational hymn, opening prayer, and a welcome from the district president. The early morning seminary class presented *The Origin of Niueans*, a sort of Niuean Hill Cumorah Pageant about how the Niueans arrived in Niue through America. They used the English *Book of Mormon Reader* for dialogue and narration. The students presented scenes from the Book of Mormon. The final scene, though out of order, was Hagoth and his people building ships and sailing away, then arriving in Niue in their old fashioned outriggers, so happy to have found land that they made merry with native dances. It was a little different than the Hill Cumorah Pageant or the Manti Pageant, but it did present the message of the Book of Mormon.

After the presentation, people were invited to visit any one of three rooms for videos and further information about the Church. We had pictures and posters on the walls of the rooms to make it a good experience for the nonmembers and hopefully excite the members about missionary work.

The first of the twenty-minute presentations was in the chapel, where we showed a portion of the October 1998 missionary broadcast about the Book of Mormon featuring Elder Henry B. Eyring. We then brought them into the cultural hall, where we'd set up a table with a 150 Niuean copies of the Book of Mormon and a picture of Christ and the Articles of Faith banded together. There were also 25 English copies of the same information.

The second area was a room focusing on the family. We had posters with quotes from the prophets concerning the importance of a good family life. We showed parts of four videos on the importance of the family and how to have a family home evening. Outside the room, we had a table set up with handouts in English and Niuean on families. We were glad that we had someone there handing them out, or the children would have taken them all.

The third area focused on genealogy. We had a "Families are Forever" poster and had sample Pedigree charts on the walls. Elder and Sister Hurd, the missionary couple working in the Family History Center in Tonga, came up with President Kivalu and brought their laptop and some disks containing Niuean genealogy. We assigned a Niuean-speaking Elder to help the people fill out the forms there. There wasn't as much business as we had hoped, but the Hurds were busy most of the time. There seemed to be a basic interest in genealogy, but it needed to be promoted, and a lot of time was spent helping people.

We wanted to subtly reemphasize that Christ is the center of the gospel, so we clustered eight or ten pictures of Christ on the wall. We also had a large "Purpose of Life" sign with accompanying handouts on the table below it, as well as small posters of each page of the handout taped to the wall. We also scattered different Mormonad signs around the rooms.

We intended to have the people move to another section after twenty minutes, but decided instead to go ahead with the light refreshments and have the next session while some of the people ate. It was a good decision as some of the people had been there for quite some time.

We served "light refreshments," which meant heaps and heaps of cookies and sweets. We showed videos in the cultural hall while the food was being served to make as much as we could out of the time we had with these people. "Unto This End Was I Born" was followed by "Man's Search for Happiness" and "Elaine Dart," a video about a woman with cerebral palsy who does everything with her feet. The people were fascinated with this video. They couldn't believe that someone would be that persistent.

The open house was an overwhelming success. The members really came through in bringing their friends. We had a standing room only crowd of over 200 people there, and more than 60 were nonmembers. We now understood why the Prophet had encouraged the members to not stay paused on some plateaus but to move forward in a major way in having activities like open houses.

General Authority Visit

❖

Establishing His Church is a unique assignment. We must take the gospel of Jesus Christ to all people in their own language without defiling the purity of the message. The Church must help develop leaders of integrity, leaders from whom honest people everywhere can receive inspired guidance. . . . The Church must teach correct laws and ordinances, in the Lord's way, which qualify the obedient believer for eternal life. There are many other requirements familiar to us that make the task of establishing such a Church seem overwhelming, but such is the assignment from the Lord.

Elder Earl M. Monson, "Establishing the Church," *Ensign*, Nov. 1998

The open house was so successful that President Kivalu requested that we plan another for the district conference when a member of our Area Presidency, Elder Earl M. Monson, and his wife would be present. We put together for the visit a number of activities to raise the profile of the Church in Niue, including a visit with the Premier, a tour of the prison, and a national Songfest.

Premier Visit

On the first day of Elder Monson's visit, we toured all of the Church properties and then called on the Niuean Premier's office. We were escorted into Premier Sani Lakatani's office and told we had about one hour of visiting time with him. He apologized that he would not be able to attend the Songfest in the evening, but told us that he would accept our invitation to attend the district conference Sunday morning. Elder Monson discussed some of the things that the Church was doing worldwide and told him about the worldwide general conference that had just been held.

In the early afternoon, the district presidency met with Elder Monson and President Kivalu for some training and a review of the conference agendas. Elder Monson gave some good instruction concerning the two major concerns of the first presidency, the youth and missionary work. We then returned home and began to make the final preparations for the Songfest.

Songfest

In the evening we held the First Annual Niue Youth Songfest. It was a smashing success. President Haioti claimed that 378 people attended, but we think it was closer to 300. No matter what the number, it was a great night. When you realize that there were only about 1500 people living in the country, you understand what a success the event was. We had prepared a simple program to hand out to the attendees and a schedule for when each group was to sing. After fourteen groups, we ended up only five minutes behind schedule. We had one group from each of our four branches, and the other ten were youth from other religious denominations. About half of them were from the LMS or Ekalesia Church. We would have had sixteen groups, but a member of the Catholic Church passed away, and a number of the Apostolic Church's group came down with the flu. We had over 200 nonmembers in our meetinghouse—160 on chairs in the cultural hall and the rest sitting sideways in the chapel pews, and there were heaps more outside on the veranda. We were surprised, though, at how few of the parents came to see their children perform. At least 200 youth performed, averaging 15 people per group. Two large LMS groups had some very good counter beats. All of our branch groups sang in English, and most of the other groups sang in Niuean.

At the conclusion, Elder Monson made some remarks about using music and good songs to replace unrighteous thoughts. He said that bad and good thoughts couldn't coexist, so an uplifting song is a good replacement for a bad thought. After the program we had a very nice assortment of refreshments, which was a big hit with the kids. It was much better treatment than they usually got at other youth activities in the country. Our own youth were very excited about it because the other kids at school keep telling them that they were coming to the Mormon Church to sing. The Songfest had really picked up momentum after we'd posted colored signs in the town center and on store windows. President Haioti later told us that people had complimented him on how good the program was and especially on how smoothly things went.

We again set up a display table with copies of the Book of Mormon, pictures of Christ, *For the Strength of Youth* pamphlets, and Articles of Faith cards in Niuean. Only 30 copies of the Book of Mormon were taken this time, but many of the pictures of Christ were taken. As we took Elder and Sister Monson through the village of Tamakautonga on the way back to their hotel, a mother and three children waved and smiled at us from the roadside. No one in Tamakautonga had ever done that before. It was a small thing, but a move in the right direction.

Each youth that participated got a nice certificate of participation to hang on their wall. It wasn't fancy, but it did say that it was sponsored by The Church of Jesus Christ of Latter-day Saints. We thought that it would be a good way to get the Church's name in the homes of the people.

Prison Visit

Saturday was the beginning of district conference, and we had a priesthood leadership meeting and a women's meeting running simultaneously in the morning with the district and branch council meetings scheduled for the late afternoon. In between these two sessions we had a very interesting experience. I don't know why, but when we were making the agenda a request was made from the mission president to visit the Church members who were in jail. I told them we had no members in prison, but we kept the visit on the agenda. When we arrived at 3:00 p.m., all seven of the prisoners were dressed in nice clothes. We formed a little seating area, and President Kivalu, fluent in Niuean from his mission, spoke to the prisoners. Then Elder Monson offered a special prayer for them. It's strange to say, but there was a very strong spirit there. When we had completed our part, the prisoners took out their musical instruments—a guitar, a ukulele, and an eight-stringed mandolin-like instrument—and sang us two religious songs. One of the prisoners, a former minister who was serving time for vehicular manslaughter while drunk, made a few remarks. It was a very touching and uplifting visit, and I kept thinking of the words of the Savior, "I was in prison, and ye came unto me. . . . Inasmuch as ye have done it unto one of the least of these my brethren, ye have done it unto me." (Matt. 25: 36, 40) It felt to me like we had truly ministered unto the Savior himself. As we were leaving, the men ran to their prison garden and picked some cabbage and onions to give to us.

Convert Baptism

After the prison visit, we went to the chapel for the baptism of a fourteen-year-old young man. He'd been taught in the branch president's home because he was a friend of the branch president's fourteen-year-old son. Elder Monson was asked to make some comments during the baptism, and he told an interesting story about the baptism of his great-grandfather. It seems that he was working in a prison in Norway taking food to the prisoners. Two Mormon missionaries had been jailed for their religious activities, and while he fed them, they taught him the gospel. When he accepted their challenge to be baptized, he secured the prison keys and let them out. They baptized him, and when it was over, they returned to the prison cell and he locked them up again. This story brought to mind the experience of Paul and Silas who where cast into prison and converted the jailor. (See Acts 16: 19-40)

Government Officials at District Conference

We had issued special invitations to all of the members of the National Assembly, the cabinet ministers, and the Premier to attend the Songfest and the general session of district conference so they could hear Elder Monson speak. None of the government officials attended the Songfest because of a cocktail party on a New Zealand naval boat that night, but Premier Sani Lakatani and one of the Cabinet Ministers, Dion Taufitu, did attend the general session of our conference. Two of the Premier's brothers are bishops in Hawaii, and his son is a returned missionary. Many of Minister Taufitu's family are also members, and he had, a number of years ago, regularly fed the people that constructed our chapel in his village.

President Kivalu presented the Premier with a brand-new leather-bound quadruple combination that President Kivalu had just purchased for himself. It was a nice gesture on his part and very quick thinking. We invited both of them to join us for lunch after the conference, but they had other commitments.

Conclusion of District Conference

After lunch, a temple fireside was held. Elder Monson had been involved with the temple construction department before his call to be a general authority, so he had many spiritual experiences about the modern construction of temples to share with the members. He encouraged the members to prepare to go to the temple and to have a recommend even though they could not attend the temple often. We went directly from the fireside to the airport, and the visitors flew home. It was a wonderful district conference weekend that uplifted us as well as all of the members of the district. It was a very memorable first experience of spending so much friendly time with a general authority and his wife.

Government and Community Involvement

> *. . . as in the past, we urge members of the Church to be full participants in political, governmental, and community affairs. Members of the Church are under special obligations to seek out and then uphold those leaders who are wise, good, and honest (see D&C 98:10). Thus, we strongly urge men and women to be willing to serve on school boards, city and county councils and commissions, state legislatures, and other high offices of either election or appointment, including involvement in the political party of their choice.*

First Presidency letter, 15 Jan. 1998, quoted in "Getting Involved, Giving Service, Growing," *Ensign*, Feb. 1999, 21

Niue has a democratically elected parliamentary government. A premier chosen by the vote of twenty elected representatives in the Fale Fono, or Niuean Assembly, serves as the head of government. While Niue is self-governing and fully responsible for all internal affairs, its purse strings and external affairs are controlled by New Zealand.

Each village elects its own village council, which receives grants from the national government to fund development projects. Village councils also organize show days and conduct fundraisers to generate revenue for village activities.

Many of the church members were full participants in political, governmental, and community affairs and played significant roles and made meaningful contributions in the Niuean government. Lagavalu Haioti, president of the Alofi Niue District served as commissioner of the Niue High Court and was the highest-ranking Niuean judge. He started serving as a part-time justice of the peace in 1975 while he was teaching school and the senior magistrate of the court. In his role as commissioner of the Niue High Court, he was responsible for 50 land commissioner judges and six justices of the peace. He also served as the chairman of Forestry Projects, the chairman of Savings and Loan Society (the government credit union), and had been clerk of the Alofi South Village Council for 12 years.

Sister Veve Jacobsen, a Relief Society teacher in the Alofi South Branch, was a member of the National Assembly and in every election she polled either the first or second largest number of votes of those elected. She not only served as a member of the assembly, but also as the Minister of Health and Education, one of the premier's three cabinet ministers. She also served as deputy premier, a position that brought her acclaim as the highest-ranking female government official in Niuean history.

Other Church members, in addition to Sister Jacobsen, also had served in the nation's National Assembly: Liumaihetau Matagi served in the Assembly for 12 years, Fumaka Molai, one of our full-time missionaries, represented his village for nine years and Makamau Hekau served one three-year term.

Another woman of prominence in the Niuean government was Sister Maihetoe Hekau, who served as the chairwoman of the Public Service Commission-which had responsibility for hiring, promotion, training and salary of all government workers.

Also holding a number of prominent positions in Niuean government was Laga Lavini, president of the Niue South Branch. He was the general manager of the Niue International Airport, fire chief and a member of the Alofi South Town Council. He also served as a member of the Civil Aviation Advisory Committee and was treasurer of the Niue Public Service Association. I wrote about the Niuean members activities in their national government in the *Church News* on 18 September 1999, entitled "Church Grows Prominent on Coral Atoll of Pacific."

Scripture at National Assembly

Because the Church members were heavily involved in local and national government affairs, Sandy and I were granted opportunities to participate in some government activities. For example, one day we received a call from the secretary of the National Assembly inquiring whether we had received our invitation to attend the opening of the National Assembly. We had not. She informed us that one would be sent over so we could attend the opening the next morning. She said that they wanted me to represent The Church of Jesus Christ of Latter-day Saints in giving a Bible reading, and I could choose the text. Because of the reputation of the new Premier and many of the National Assembly members, I chose the entire thirteenth chapter of Romans.

It was a fun experience to represent the Church at the opening of the National Assembly. They had four religions participate: us, the Catholics, the Seventh-day Adventists and, of course, the LMS, the dominant Church in Niue. They had two ministers participating, one giving the closing prayer and another giving a talk. They both spoke in Niuean. I read my scripture in English, as did the Seventh-day Adventist pastor. The Catholic Priest gave the opening prayer in English, too. The Seventh-day Adventist pastor and the Catholic priest were both Tongans. We thought it quite funny that at the opening of the Niuean assembly, the first three participants were all connected with Tonga. The other missionary couple, the Molais, were also invited because he had previously served as a member of the assembly for nine years.

Government Support of London Missionary Society

I was also invited to attend a government meeting concerning the hiring of full-time ministers at the primary school and the high school. I was the only person there representing a Church other than the LMS. The meeting gave me the feeling that the government was reverting back to the old days of a state religion. The LMS Church was having a hard time because many of their kids were staying home and watching

TV instead of coming to church. The government currently allowed only LMS pastors to teach religion for two hours a week at the school. The government now wanted to pay two ministers to be at the schools full-time to teach every day. The teachers were opposed—they couldn't legally lengthen the school day, and they already didn't have enough time to do all that they were supposed to do. Basically, the government leaders at the meeting said that it didn't matter what the teachers or administrators wanted—they were there to do what the community told them to do. It boiled down to another way to funnel money into the LMS Church and their ministers. I tried not to say too much in the meeting because I was a foreigner, and they were trying to make the country more Niuean. I did, however, tell them about our very successful early morning seminary program and suggested that they consider having the students come to school early for their religious education. Afterwards, I told District President Haioti that we should write a letter to the Cabinet Minister for Religion, who was promoting the LMS proposal, and let him know that we were against it unless they allowed us to educate our students separately.

One of our members had represented the primary school at a previous meeting concerning this same issue. She told me privately that the LMS leaders wanted to know how the Mormons were able to do so well teaching their children all about the Bible and God.

There was no one representing any other Church at this first meeting, even though the Council of Churches is supposedly deciding it. After the meeting, Sandy and I visited the ministers of three other Churches and asked if they had been invited. Each one responded that they had not but would have gone if they had been. The minutes of an earlier meeting indicated that the government planned on giving $50,000 to the LMS and providing three scholarships to send young people to be trained to be ministers. My comment to the members was that maybe the Mormons should apply for one of the scholarships to pay for one of our youth's mission. I also told our members if they try to set up full-time ministers in the schools I would ask the Church to provide two school teachers to serve as teaching missionaries without charge to the government.

Fortunately, the proposal was never enacted, though the government did give $50,000 to the LMS. Our members were very upset with the payment and felt that some money should also be given to the Church, but, of course, the Church doesn't accept such payments from governments.

Official Representative of Niue to US Government

Sandy and I were extremely impressed by the significant public service of the members of the Church in Niue and felt a strong desire to assist these people we loved so much. So at the conclusion of our mission in Niue I fashioned a plan to help the people of Niue. Since we lived in the Washington, DC area, I felt that I might be able to establish a relationship between Niue and some of the agencies of the U.S. government. I thought that this could best be accomplished by approaching the Premier about appointing me as the Official Representative of Niue to the US Government. I meet with the Premier and discussed the idea with him and how I could possibly find some ways for them to get assistance from the US Government. I told him that I would do this at no charge because of my great love for the people of his country. I knew the Territorial Representative from American Samoa to the US Congress and knew that he would be willing to work with them as another country in the South Pacific. When we were released from our mission in Niue the Premier did draft a letter appointing me as the Official Representative of Niue to the US Government.

My role as the official representative did not turn out like I envisioned. I returned to our home in Fairfax, Virginia one of the suburbs of Washington, DC and met with the Territorial Representative from Samoa and formulated with him some plans about assisting Niue but could not get the Niuean Premier to move forward and my role as I had envisioned died an unfortunate death.

I did not view this as a failure in my attempt to make a difference. It was part of our missionary role to be anxiously engaged in good causes and leave the area we were serving a better place. We were taking our cue from the examples of the members of the Church and the urging of the First Presidency of the Church to be full participants in political, governmental, and community affairs.

Memory Bank of Unusual Experiences in Niue

❖

Certainly the most successful lives are those that have the most worthwhile experiences. . . . The purpose of the Church is to help us translate the principles of the gospel of Christ into constructive, meaningful human experience. And everyone should work toward this end by a daily practice of thinking some uplifting thoughts, listening to some fine music, reading some stimulating literature, doing some good deeds, and having some great experiences every day.

Sterling W. Sill, "Great Experiences," *Ensign*,
June 1971

It seemed like each day of our mission we were experiencing peculiar occurrences that we deposited in our memory bank. After a while we realized that many of the memorable moments of our mission that were placed in our memory bank were not the advertised ones, not the conversions, reactivations, or goals we achieved. They were much less prepossessing. They came to the door of our memory unannounced and simply never left. Many of these were photographs taken by our hearts and videos recorded in our minds that made special moments last forever. As I look back in a reminiscent mood upon the events in Niue that have crowded my mind I realize how cherished, amusing, and unusual many of our experiences in Niue were.

Mormon Trail

We learned by experience that the roadmaps of Niue were not very accurate. This was especially true when we tried to take shortcuts, but whenever we found a road that we hadn't traveled on and had a little extra time, we would take it to see how it could be used to our advantage in the future.

Returning from a preparation day caving trip in the van, we took a dirt road into the woods. Halfway up we saw another road that went off to the right in the direction we wanted to go. After driving for a while on this road, we came upon a tree with a white sign that said *Nauvoo*. We went a little farther and found another sign that said *Ohio*, which was soon followed by *Illinois* and *Iowa*. We began looking for wagon trains. About this time we entered a dense forest on a narrow, not-well-traveled road. We soon came upon a tree that had fallen across the road. The missionaries and two young men that were with us tried to remove it. When they'd broken a few branches off, it looked like I could drive around it, but the left front wheel got stuck in a mud hole, just like in the film *Legacy*. We were reliving the pioneer days. We had traveled from Nauvoo to Iowa and we were freeing our wagon from the muddy trail. With the help of some logs and sticks we were eventually able to continue our journey. The road ultimately ended at the back of the elementary school—far from our destination. Finding these signs on an isolated back road in Niue was a total surprise but also a testimony of the level of youth activities on the island. We were never able to obtain a complete account of the original event, but the signs were part of a pioneer experience for the Church's sesquicentennial.

Insects, Mice, Geckos, and the Food Chain

We had many experiences observing the food chain as missionaries. When we woke up one morning in Niue, we found that something had eaten through two plastic bags to get to our oatmeal and another plastic bag to sample the taco seasoning packet that we'd brought from America. It was obviously something bigger than a cockroach. The next day it ate through a plastic lid to get to the oatmeal. We were sure it was a mouse.

We put out some poison mouse cookies that were so virulent we had to purchase them from the hospital. Sure enough, when we got up on Wednesday morning, there was the mouse up on the shelf staring at us. It had barely nibbled on the cookies, and it didn't even run away until I chased it. Thursday morning it was on the shelf again, watching us when we got up. While it was sitting there, a cockroach came running by, and the mouse just lifted up its head and ate it. We couldn't figure out which was worse, the cockroach or the mouse. We would prefer not to have either. Later, Sandy went into the kitchen to fix breakfast, and a gecko walked by with a dead cockroach in its mouth. This was after we had sprayed bug killer, mind you. That night, however, the mouse gnawed through the container with the poison cookies—it was pretty determined to die. The cookies must have been addictive. We waited for the corpse to stink so we could find it. When the smell finally came we found the little body under a bed in a guest bedroom, though it was harder to locate than we'd thought it would be.

Potato Soup and the Gecko

One night Sandy cooked some potato soup for dinner. We were looking forward to it since we'd found sour cream and nice potatoes at the local store that day and we hadn't had them in over a year. The potato soup was cooling in an open pan on the stove before we ate. When Sandy went to stir it, she found a dead *moko* or gecko right on top of the soup. It must have fallen off the ceiling. We weren't sure if its death was a commentary on the soup's heat or on its taste. We wondered whether to throw away the precious, hard-to-get soup or just take the gecko out. It was an easy decision. We just fished the gecko out and ate the soup. It was still delicious, and it let us know that we were truly adjusted to missionary life.

Creating a Jerky Market

Chris and Gwen Fuller, friends from Virginia, had an impact on the economy in Niue without even knowing it. We received a package of beef jerky from the Fullers shortly after the first of the year, and sometime later we had a nonmember family, the Cullings, over for dinner. They were of the Bahai faith and had a small butcher business. We had them sample the jerky, and they liked it so they decided to make some and see how it did in the market. They had us sample the first batch, as we are obviously connoisseurs of fine jerky, and give them our comments. They soon had small packages of homemade jerky selling very well. A single gift from a friend affected a whole nation.

Net Ball

Some Saturday mornings we watched the girls play net ball, a Niuean variant of basketball that's played outside on grass, concrete, or asphalt courts divided into thirds. Players are assigned to each of the divided areas and must not leave that area to pursue the ball. There are no backboards, just a hoop extended from the top of an iron pole set in a tire base. There's no dribbling the ball; only a single step may be taken while passing or shooting, and the ball must leave the player's hands before her foot hits the ground. Shots can only be blocked by reaching, not jumping. All ages played in a competition once a year. The high school girls had village teams, but the younger kids only had their sports day teams. We enjoyed watching the village girls play this interesting game.

Involvement with the Schools

There were six elementary schools and one high school on the island. Schooling was compulsory, secular, and free for all children ages five to fourteen. At more advanced grades, instruction was delivered in English. The curriculum was modeled on that used in New Zealand but also included materials designed for Pacific Islanders. While we'd been involved with the elementary school in Ha'afeva, in Niue we dealt with the high school. We did not have an opportunity to teach any religious classes like the LMS did, because there was a very well organized seminary program operated by the district that did not rely upon the full-time missionaries, which meant that mostly we attended school activities. We were asked to participate in a few activities at the school, with Sandy serving as a judge at the annual speech competition, and I was a special guest speaker for National Grandparent Day. We felt privileged, as non-Niueans, to be granted these honors.

The best event, though, was the National Primary School Sports

Day in Alofi. This is one of the big events of the year, and everyone on the island attended. The program started with a few speeches, and then each of the four teams marched in and did some fancy drill maneuvers to compete for marching excellence. A number of short-distance races and some more unusual events followed, including stilt races (those kids were fast), spear throwing (judged by where the point of the spear stopped sliding across the ground), and coconut shell races. In the coconut shell race, each child had two coconut halves connected by a large string. They stood with one foot on each coconut half with the string running from the coconut half to their hands. Keeping the string taut helped keep the coconut under their feet as they hopped to the finish line. It was a lot like kids walking on smashed tin cans. Some of the kids could really sprint through the event. The coconut frond race, on the other hand, was an event for teams of three. A coconut frond is the stem that coconuts grown on. Part of it is shaped like a round ski. One team member would stand on the frond and hold a pole in front of him. His two teammates take hold of the ends of the pole and run, pulling the third person along on his coconut-frond skis. It was a very fun race to watch. The coconut bud throw was interesting as well. When coconuts first develop, they are small, round, and soft. The children take this small coconut bud and insert the stems of coconut leaves in one end like feathers in a bird's tail. They compete to see who can throw them the farthest.

The great thing was that everyone participated, not just the super athletes. The little first graders did everything the big kids did. It was like a miniature Olympics, complete with pedestals for first, second, and third place. The kids didn't have to wait long for their awards; they went straight from the finish line to the stand to receive their medals. We took many pictures of the participating Church kids. It was a very fun day.

Government Charges Against Member

While we were in Niue, one of our single adult brethren was charged with the attempted rape of a woman in the US Peace Corps. The case became a big issue because of the Peace Corps involvement. He pleaded not guilty, which was unusual in Niue—most defendants plead guilty and are given very light sentences. It was all the more interesting because the counsel for the defense wasn't a lawyer. Steve Jefferson was a New Zealander handyman mechanic who had married a Niuean. He took the case because he wanted to help a fellow Church member and no one else would represent him.

The first thing Steve did was petition the High Court of New Zealand to grant bail to the accused after the local court had not granted bail. The chief of police, who also served as the prosecuting attorney, asked the high court to then impose a curfew on him from six p.m. to nine a.m. We went to hear the proceedings because of the members involved. Since a Peace Corps woman was involved, they sent a Peace Corps area administrator up from Tonga. We knew both her and the Peace Corps woman and talked with them before the trial began.

The trial was a bit anticlimactic—it started with the judge telling the chief of police that the local court didn't have jurisdiction. Instead, the judge of the High Court of New Zealand that periodically visits Niue had to hear it because of the innocent plea. The chief of police confirmed this with Attorney General Warner Banks (no relation to us) over a recess, then asked for a continuation of the bail and curfew provisions. The non-lawyer counsel Steve Jefferson reminded the judge that the bail order had lapsed two weeks ago, and that the defendant hadn't done anything wrong during that time. He didn't think the restrictions should be reinstated. The judge was upset that the chief hadn't told him about this lapse in his initial request. The judge and his two assistants went into conference and concluded that the bail and curfew provisions would not be reinstated. The Peace Corps boss was livid. She felt that the young woman needed protection and that the court was imperiling her by not reinstating these restrictions. The boss told the young woman that she would take her back to Tonga on the next plane for her protection. The young Peace Corps worker broke down and sobbed because she didn't want to leave. Her boss rushed her away in a rage. We visited with the Peace Corps woman before she returned to Tonga, and she told us she hadn't wanted a federal case—she'd just wanted his hand slapped quickly. At this point, she just wanted the case to be over.

In the end, our member was cleared of the attempted rape charge, though he received a strong reprimand for peeking in the young woman's window. The Peace Corps member was transferred from Niue and wasn't replaced while we were in Niue.

Sunday Airplanes

The biggest happening on the island was the weekly coming and going of the airplane. Everyone on the island was at the airport on Sunday whether they knew someone who was travelling or not—it was just the place to be. It was nothing to have over 200 at the airport for only twenty passengers getting on or off the plane. Church—of any denomination—was of secondary importance at that hour. The ministers of all the churches in Niue complained about the Sunday airline schedule. They found it quite hypocritical that Tonga wouldn't let a flight land at their airport on Sunday because it would break the Sabbath, but didn't have any problem sending a flight across the international date line to land somewhere else where it was Sunday. They didn't fly on Sunday in their country, just in other countries. Basically, Tonga followed the letter of the law and not the spirit so that they could follow the law of money.

Priesthood Blessing

We had been to the hospital frequently over the previous two weeks because various members had been there for high blood pressure, diabetes, maternity, and other things. One day we went to the hospital as usual and visited with the nonmember mother of one of our district councilors. She had been in and out of the hospital frequently over the last two weeks. The Molais were visiting her as well—Elder Molai had lived with her family as a young boy. He was excited to see me and asked that I assist him in giving her a priesthood blessing. One of her inactive sons, who was the minister of the largest congregation of the LMS in Alofi, was waiting outside. Elder Molai wanted me to seal the anointing, but I told him that he should do it because he was very close to her. However, I felt very strongly at the time that we should ask the Lord to take her before she started to suffer. She was not well, but was talking and communicating with the family. Elder Molai did not ask the Lord to let her be taken, but he did ask that she be given peace. When we returned home, I still had the strong feeling that we should have asked the Lord to take her from this earthly life, so when we offered our family prayer that night, I prayed that the Lord would grant her leave of this life. The next day, Sandy came to me and said, "Did you know that she died this morning and that the funeral service is to be held at 3:30 p.m. today?" We knew that our prayer had been answered, and we learned again that whatsoever thing we ask for that is right will be granted.

Our memory bank was filled with many of these kinds of memories. Many did not linger in our memory bank because of lessons that we learned from them. Rather they found a place in our heart and we shared them with friends and family when we returned home. I assume that this is similar to the experiences that many senior missionaries have during their period of service and they share them because their picture is planted firmly in their hearts and minds. And like the wise man Solomon from Ecclesiastes, "My heart had great experience." (Ecclesiastes 1:16)

Preparation Day Catastrophe

❖

I want to make it clear that I am not adverse to some recreation. All work and no play makes Jack a dull boy, and likewise Jill a dull doll. But when it becomes an end in itself, then we are in danger. We cannot expect to refine the substance of character from "the husks of pleasure."

President Gordon B. Hinckley, "Cornerstones as Stepping Stones," BYU Commencement Address, April 20, 1979

Preparation day is a break from the vigorous proselyting routine that allows missionaries to take care of personal matters so they can give their full attention to missionary service the rest of the week. The missionary handbook says that these personal matters would include washing clothes, getting a haircut, cleaning house, shopping, and other personal matters. It is the suggested time to write letters to family and friends. It is also a time for recreational and cultural activities, such as visiting museums, art galleries, historical sites, zoos, special exhibits, and cultural centers.

Niue offered a large variety of recreational activities, most of them free for missionaries. There were many caves, chasms, sea tracks, lookouts, forests, snorkeling, scuba, and whale watching spots, and even some very small but beautiful little beaches. While the water activities were prohibited for young full-time missionaries they were not prohibited for senior missionaries. Our preparation day activities often involved visiting the spectacular caves, chasms, and sea tracks. Some of these beautiful places were easy to access, so we usually took our visitors there. Many of these caves had giant window openings on to the flat reef, beautiful ocean backdrops, and stalactites and stalagmites of many variegated colors. Many had crystal clear seawater pools full of brilliantly colored tiny fish. It was like viewing a mini aquarium. The place we visited most often was the Limu pool because it had a peaceful, relaxing panoramic view of beautiful, clear, blue water—and it was easy to access.

Another favorite area was the Togo Chasm, which I called the Grand Canyon of Niue. Going there was a day-long activity. We had to walk through the very thick Huvalu rainforest where tree roots criss-crossed the pathway making the path very hazardous. The path emerges from the forest to a panoramic view of beautiful sculptured sea corals rising in sharp slabs and pinnacles like five-foot razor blades. There was a concrete walkway lined with rope fencing to hold onto as you walked. It would have looked like the moon if there had been no vegetation. After hiking this trail for a half hour, we descended down a huge thirty-two-rung ladder to get to a very small, sandy beach. It took a long time, but it was worth it.

Catastrophe Strikes

When we had Church visitors from overseas we would frequently use part of the day for preparation day activities. In June 1999, Elder Talmage Shill, the Area Doctor for the South Pacific Area, came to Niue to visit the medical facilities with his wife and Elder Schuenman from the mission office. When we had finished visiting the hospital facilities and doctors, we decided to visit one of the caves. Elder Shill was not really dressed for it because he was wearing slippery leath-er-bottomed shoes, but he felt that he would be ok and insisted that we go ahead and visit the two caves at Avaiki. To get there, we had to hike down a very difficult rocky area and then cross an exposed reef at low tide. We had to be careful not to get our feet caught in one of the indentions in the coral. We arrived at a big cave that had one of the beautiful blue pools with colorful tropical fish.

Elder Shill was doing well until he started walking away from the pool. His foot slipped and wedged in one of the coral crevasses, and he fell hard. He immediately knew that his leg was broken. In great pain, he moved his left leg out of the hole and tried to straighten it out. His wife and Sandy made him comfortable, and Elder Schuenman and I gave him a priesthood blessing. As soon as the blessing was over, I took off running to find a phone to call the hospital. Luckily, unlike Ha'afeva, many individual residences in Niue have phones, and after trying a few homes I found one with a phone and called the hospital. I gave the ambulance directions and ran back to check on Elder Shill. The ambulance was quick to respond. They gave Elder Shill some pain medication and sent someone back to get a stretcher.

Now came the difficult, harrowing task of getting a man on a stretcher across the coral reef, then up, over and under large boulders, and through very narrow passages to the ambulance. I ran to the village and got some of the men to help us carry him. While climbing down the narrow passages was difficult it was an almost impossible task to take a man on a stretcher through some of the narrow passageways. Even with their help, moving Elder Shill required a lot of stretcher transfers from one set of hands to another and we had to a rest a number of times and catch our breath.

While Niue is a very small country, they had a very well equipped hospital with qualified doctors, unlike remote Ha'afeva. They took an X-ray and confirmed that the femur had a long vertical break that would require surgery to repair. He needed to go to New Zealand.

The Lord had prepared a way. The only plane that week would be arriving from Samoa that very night on its way to Auckland. We discussed the situation with Air New Zealand, and they decided to remove one of the front seats in the plane and strap him in a stretcher on the floor since he couldn't bend his leg. When we arrived at the airport they had to use a fork lift to get him to the door of the plane. The pilot balked, however, and said that he would not allow Elder Shill to lie on the floor because it was too dangerous. The plane was full, but they moved someone and had Elder Shill sit up with his leg stretched out into the aisle. This was extremely painful, but the doctors gave him a lot of pain medication to take on the four-hour flight. Elder Shill, his wife, and Elder Schuenman flew back to New Zealand with firsthand knowledge of the Niue medical system. They also knew that while Elder Shill had faced adversity, the priesthood blessing given him had been fulfilled, and the Lord had been with him and comforted him through this difficult ordeal.

Gone from Ha'afeva but Not Forgotten

❖

There is something in man, an essential part of his mind, which recalls the events of the past. . . . He may have a lapse of memory; he may not be able to recall at the moment things that he knows or words that he has spoken; he may not have the power at his will to call up these events and words; but let God Almighty touch the mainspring of the memory, and awaken recollection, and you will find then that you have not even forgotten . . .

President Joseph F. Smith, *Gospel Doctrine*, Deseret Book Co., 1939, 311

Even though we were transferred to the country of Niue, we did not forget our beloved friends in Ha'afeva. Truly, the mainspring of my memory awakened my recollection of many uplifting and faith-promoting experiences that we enjoyed during our eleven months with those members. Two community initiatives that we started before we left were completed after our transfer, and the results were better than we could have expected.

Hospital Service Project

Our first service project in Ha'afeva was to clean the little four-room hospital. There is no way to describe the condition it was in. There was no running water because the government had never bothered to put rain gutters on the building that would flow to the sima next to the building. The beds had no mattresses, and the window in that room was almost rusted away. We were afraid that even touching that window would make it fall out, leaving no protection at all from the elements. The floors were filthy. The only crib in the clinic was falling apart. Sandy found a big bundle of sugar and a bag of crackers in an examining room drawer. There were, of course, bugs in all of it.

In our service project, two of the brethren fixed the crib. They also fixed a door that was hanging by a single hinge so that it would open and close most of the way. Finally, we discarded all the broken floor tiles. The hospital was much improved after our service but still far from being hospitable.

We had a second branch service project to clean up the hospital grounds. It was also very successful, and the grounds were as much improved as the interior. The village seemed to be taking better care of the clinic since we'd cleaned it. As part of the outside work, we fixed up the fence along the road, standing up posts and reconnecting them with barbed wire. It took a dozen people a little more than three hours, and most of them felt very good about doing the service.

We then proposed a plan to get funding from our home ward in Oakton, Virginia, to fix up the interior tile and repaint the clinic before we left the island. Our ward raised $600, but we left Ha'afeva without starting the project. The PBO promised that they would replace all floor tiles and then do whatever else they could with the money that was left.

We shed tears of joy in Niue when we received word that the PBO had sent some men to Ha'afeva and not only replaced all the tile, but also replaced all the rusted out louver windows with left over windows from chapels. Hoa Fonua, the man in charge of contract work, said the men felt so badly about how the dirty walls looked next to the new windows and tile that they called the mission office and used some leftover money to buy some paint that was on sale and send it on the next boat so the interior could be painted. They said the hospital looked like new when they were finished. This labor had been free of charge, donated by the PBO of Tonga. All of this was done thanks to the generosity and love of the members of the Oakton Ward.

Eagle Book Project

Another Oakton Ward member, Michael Wheatley, served the Lulunga District through his Eagle Scout service project. He organized his family and friends to collect and ship school books to the elementary schools in the Lulunga District. We were notified in Niue by the mission office that the shipment had arrived in Nuku'alofa but unfortunately, the project looked like it might be frustrated by the duty fees. I wrote to several well-placed friends in Tonga, including the Governor of Ha'apai, asking for help in getting the books off the boat and into the hands of the people who needed them without the extra expense of duty fees. As we were preparing to leave Niue at the end of our mission, I unexpectedly received the following email message from the mission office:

We spent time today looking for your lost boxes of books. Paul from the warehouse finally said, he was sure they were still in one of the containers that is unopened, that will be put in the covered warehouse tomorrow and separated. We planned to go again tomorrow. Then at 5:30 PM, a call came from the governor of Ha'apai saying the container was at the Ha'apai wharf and they need some kind of paperwork or information from you. Please FAX the wharf in Ha'apai at 60-004 to resolve this. I have no idea how the shipment got from Tongatapu to Ha'apai.

The Lord stepped in, and the books had somehow appeared on the wharf in Pangai, Ha'apai, where we wanted them. This news was not the end of the story. We sent the requested information, but we were informed that a duty would still have to be paid for the books even though they were to be a gift for government schools. Fortunately, we had to return to Tonga to report on Niue to the mission president, so we were able to take care of this when we returned to Tongatapu. We had to go to the parliament building while the Parliament was in session and find Governor Fielakepa of Ha'apai. We were able to make contact with him during a recess, and he assured us that he would personally take care of the books and see that they were distributed to the elementary schools in the Lulunga District. A few weeks after we arrived home in Virginia, we received a personal letter from Governor Fielakepa informing us that he had done so and that his own mother, one of the retired heads of education in Tonga, sorted and allocated the books among the schools herself. It was icing on the cake at the end of our mission.

We learned from these two projects that there is an opportunity for those at home to help in the senior missionary work in various ways. Even being far away did not limit the good that our own ward members were able to do through these two projects. They had prayed and fasted about our drought and now they had used their resources and time to bless the lives of the people in our mission.

The Sun Sets on
Our Mission

❖

Missions are for missionaries. It is a marvelous gift of time, a time given when you can experience glimpses of heavenly life here on earth. It is a time of cleansing and refreshing. It is a special time when the Holy Ghost can seal upon you the knowledge of the great plan for your exaltation. It is one of your best opportunities to become a celestial candidate.

Elder William R. Bradford, "Sanctification through Missionary Service," *Ensign*, Nov. 1981

As our mission drew to a close, the pace of events seemed to accelerate. Every day seemed so short, every hour so fleeting. Truly, the time was moving on wings of lightning. With ever-increasing speed we chased the sunset, thinking that if we kept up with it, it would extend our mission indefinitely and that the curtain would not be drawn on the last act of our senior missionary service. We wanted to continue glimpsing heavenly life.

As we reviewed our mission, we realized that many of our experiences and lessons were common to all senior missionary service. We also recognized that each mission has unique challenges and opportunities that stretch and test you. Our mission was no exception. All the phantoms that frightened us before we left on our mission had now been unmasked and dismissed. The Lord truly blessed us according to our specific needs. Our unusual and rare experiences all served as building blocks for our household of faith.

Like every missionary, we experienced our share of trials and challenges. We often asked ourselves, "Why has this happened to me? As we sailed upon difficult deep seas with the billowing surges and fierce winds as our enemies, the heavens gathering blackness and all the elements seeming to hedge up our way, I recalled what the Lord counseled Joseph Smith, "Know thou, my son that all these things shall give thee experience, and shall be for thy good." (D&C 122:7) President Spencer W. Kimball said of someone who was experiencing personal trials, "God just wanted her to be polished a little more." (President Henry B. Eyring, "Mountains to Climb," *Ensign*, May 2012, 26) Truly our trials and challenges gave us great experience and polished two rough stones from Virginia a little more.

We did not succeed in changing everything we initially desired because gradually, some desires changed. Some things we'd hoped to change now seemed unimportant. We realized that it was not the right time to change some things. We learned that some good can be derived from almost every event. We especially learned that faith was more important than any other leadership quality. Our missionary life took us around the obstacles and led us past them and helped us lose sight of things that were unimportant or beyond the mark.

We learned that while the Polynesian saints are rightfully known for their deep and profound faith, they also have other, equally important qualities which characterize these Saints, such as their immense love for the missionaries. No missionary who has ever felt the love of the Polynesian people will forget it. We had truly felt of their love, and our lives were changed forever because of it.

While we could recount many stories of their immense love of the missionaries no story better illustrates this love for the missionaries than one told by President Eric B. Shumway of the Tonga Nuku'alofa Mission. In his account he tells of a visit by Elder Joseph B. Wirthlin of the Council of the Twelve to a stake conference that was celebrated by a massive feast. A few weeks later, the young Tongan missionaries enjoyed a similar massive feast for a regular zone conference. When President Shumway mentioned this to the Saints and inquired why they had done so, they answered, "You know we don't make distinctions between apostles and our own missionaries. We honor them equally." (Eric B. Shumway, *Tongan Saints, Legacy of Faith*, The Institute for Polynesian Studies, 1991, 10) We felt this same special love from the people wherever we went.

President Shumway explained the reason for this love by saying, "Although times and attitudes are changing in Tonga today, there is still a difference between Tongan and western attitudes toward poverty and wealth. The typical Westerner measures wealth by the things he or she accumulates and stores for personal use. A Tongan is wealthy in what he or she gives away. Conversely, a Westerner feels the bite of poverty in what he or she lacks personally. A Tongan suffers poverty only when he or she has nothing to give someone he or she loves. Hence the out pouring of gifts, mats, tapa cloth, food, compliments, friendship, and love upon the missionaries." (Eric B. Shumway, *Tongan Saints, Legacy of Faith*, The Institute for Polynesian Studies, 1991, 10–11)

This love is reflected in that fact that you never find someone starving or begging for food in Tonga. They take care of feeding anyone who is in need or cannot provide for themselves. Someone stated that one of the worst things that ever came to Tonga was the refrigerator—it has caused people to keep their leftovers instead of sharing them.

As we closed our mission, we thought of how our missionary service had been much like our old sixteen-foot missionary boat. There were parts of the boat that, taken by themselves, would sink. The engine by itself would sink. The propeller if unattached would sink. But when all the parts of the boat were fitted together correctly, it sailed upon the sea. So it was with our mission life. All our missionary experiences added to our life experiences formed a craft that sailed us through the stormy seas of missionary life to the safe harbor beyond.

Our blessed missionary service had surely stirred our souls. We viewed many of our sacred goals differently as we returned home. As Jeremiah said, the Lord's "word was in mine heart as a burning fire shut up in my bones," (Jeremiah 20:9) and a desire for continued missionary service burned in our bosoms. We recalled the refrain of an old hymn,

"Thy Spirit, Lord, Has Stirred Our Souls," and reflected upon how we were now a new man and woman in Christ and better celestial candidates.

> *Thy Spirit, Lord, has stirred our souls,*
> *And by its inward shining glow*
> *We see anew our sacred goals*
> *And feel thy nearness here below.*
> *No burning bush near Sinai*
> *Could show thy presence, Lord, more nigh.*
> *Did not our hearts within us burn?*
> *We know the Spirit's fire is here.*
> *It makes our souls for service yearn;*
> *It makes the path of duty clear.*
> *Lord, may it prompt us, day by day,*
> *In all we do, in all we say.*

Hymns, 1985, *Thy Spirit, Lord, Has Stirred Our Souls*, no. 157

ABOUT THE AUTHORS
Douglas W. and Sandra C. Banks

Douglas was raised in Gallup, New Mexico and Sandy in Redlands, California. They met while attending Brigham Young University and were married in the Los Angeles California Temple. They are the parents of six children and grandparents to twenty-six. They raised their family in Falls Church and Fairfax in Northern Virginia where they currently reside.

Douglas studied accounting at Brigham Young University and law at George Washington University Law School. Sandy studied elementary education at Brigham Young University.

Douglas spent his professional career working as a Certified Public Accountant specializing in taxes. He was a tax partner in the international accounting firm of Touche Ross & Co. (Now Deloitte & Touche) and then practiced privately. He has served as an officer and lecturer for the American Institute of Certified Public Accountants and many other professional organizations. He is the co-author of "Real Estate Accounting and Reporting Manual", Warren, Gorham and Lamont, 1990 and author or co-author of numerous professional articles.

Sandy spent her professional career at home nurturing, teaching and prepping their children. She served as tutor, chauffeur, event planner, chef and published her own cooking book, "Moms' Best."

Douglas served a two-and-one half year mission in the Tonga Nuku'alofa Mission, then as a High Counselor, Bishop, and District President. Sandy served as a Stake Relief Society President and in the Stake YW. Douglas and Sandy served together as senior missionaries and then as President of the Tonga Nuku'alofa Mission. They then served together as a counselor and assistant to the matron in the Washington D.C. Temple. They currently serve together in the Washington D.C. Temple as ordinance worker and sealer. Douglas also serves as the Patriarch of the Oakton Virginia Stake and Sandy as his scribe.

Made in the USA
Middletown, DE
21 March 2016